INVITE ONLY

Re-Author the Stories You Tell Yourself

JANE NJOGU SSEBUGWAWO

INDIA · SINGAPORE · MALAYSIA

ISBN 979-8-89067-862-1

Dedication

I dedicate this book to my parents, **Mr. and Mrs. Njogu** with immense gratitude and love. You have been my unwavering pillar of support throughout my life, and your belief in me has been the driving force behind my journey. I am eternally grateful for the sacrifices you have made for me. I love you both.

To my life partner, **Douglas Ssebugwawo**, your unwavering love and encouragement have been the driving force behind my journey as an author. You have been my constant cheerleader, pushing me to pursue my dreams and never giving up on me, even when I doubted myself. Thank you for being my muse, my guiding light, and my constant source of love and support. I am lucky to be doing life with you.

To **Kate Kikano** (Founder and Managing Director, TKD Lingerie): Your continuous zeal and desire to create uplifting experiences for women have played a huge role in my quest in finding meaning and understanding my passion. Having worked within the organization under your able leadership for over 5 years, I experienced first-hand the benefits of genuine service to others. Please accept my heartfelt gratitude for believing in my skills and capabilities when our paths crossed in 2017 and for being a great influence in my life.

I also dedicate this book to you who hold the desire to lead a meaningful life making conscious decisions and understanding the barriers holding you back such as existing limiting beliefs, thinking patterns, and the stories you tell yourself, there is hope and a world full of possibilities.

Contents

Acknowledgements

I would like to acknowledge the following people who played a great role in the publishing of this book:

Dr. Christine Mushibwe (Vice Chancellor of Unicaf University, Zambia): Thank you so much for accepting my request to help with the editing work. There is no way I would have managed to accomplish the feat of writing this book without you. I appreciate you, Dr. Christine.

Paul Smith (Author & Managing Director of Coaching Minds, UK): Thank you for your guidance and for being there whenever I reached out. Your support motivated me to get the book published. I appreciate you, Paul.

My Siblings & Best Friend, (Tabby, Purity, Mary, Moses & Swabrina): Thank you for your support. Each of you has played various roles in the success of this book. I am grateful that I can always count on you in my different life adventures. I love you all.

Joyceloy Kyompire & Vijaya Gowrisankar: Best Accountability Partners Ever! I appreciate you both.

To my publishers (Notion Press): I would like to thank you for your extraordinary support during the publishing stage.

Foreword

When Jane Njogu asked me to write this foreword for her first book 'Invite Only: Re-Author the Stories You Tell Yourself', I was honored and excited. Over the past year, I have been a mentor to Jane in her development as a Transformational Coach and I have seen incredible growth. When she reached out to me with her proposal and a copy of the book, I knew this was going to be something special. It is therefore with great pleasure and enthusiasm that I introduce you to the remarkable journey captured within the pages of this book.

The story of Daniella, expertly woven by, Jane Njogu, invites us to witness a profound personal transformation. Through her captivating narrative, Daniella takes us on a voyage of self-discovery, unveiling the power of embracing one's uniqueness and conquering the internal obstacles that hinder personal growth.

At the heart of this book lies the unwavering belief that we are the CEOs of our own lives. We possess the power to shape our destiny, to break free from self-imposed limitations, and to create a future filled with purpose and fulfillment. It is a reminder that our past does not define us, but rather serves as a foundation upon which we can build a brighter tomorrow.

Within these pages, you will find the wisdom and guidance of Mr. Antonio, a beacon of inspiration and a catalyst for change. His insights and thought-provoking questions challenge Daniella to confront her fears, examine her assumptions and embrace a mindset shift that empowers her to overcome obstacles with grace and resilience.

As Daniella's journey unfolds, we are reminded of the profound impact our choices and perspectives can have on our lives and the lives of those around us. Through her experiences, we discover the transformative power of positive affirmations, the importance of seeking understanding before passing judgment, and the incredible opportunities that lie within the face of adversity.

Jane Njogu, the author of this enlightening book, draws upon her own life experiences and coaching expertise to guide us on a path of self-discovery. Her words resonate with authenticity and compassion, encouraging us to embrace our uniqueness, embrace vulnerability, and to re-author our stories.

As you embark on this transformative journey, may you find inspiration, guidance, and practical wisdom within these pages. May you uncover the strength and resilience that reside within you and may you be motivated to take charge of your own life, to dream big, and pick up the pen with Jane to re-author a powerful life story.

I extend my deepest gratitude to Jane Njogu for sharing her profound insights and personal journey with us. Her commitment to empowering others and her unwavering belief in the potential for personal growth shines brightly through these words. I am confident that this book will serve many.

So, dear reader, I invite you to turn the page and immerse yourself in the transformative tale that awaits you. Embrace the lessons, reflect on your own journey, and step into the CEO role of your life.

Paul Smith, Author & Managing Director of Coaching Minds

Introduction

The town was abuzz; not only was everyone talking about it, but it was also published in every newspaper. It would be the party of the season, an exclusive, by invite only, and Daniella was the host.

Daniella lived in a small, close-knit community where everyone knew everyone. A community that held its annual festivals and meetings in their town halls where every household would have a representative. because if not, it was highly likely that everyone would want to attend. A community where a tourist or a new member would easily be identified from the crowd because they stood out like a sore thumb. A community where crime was unheard of, and the local police ensured nothing threatened the peace. The police also helped the elderly with grocery shopping and responded to minor emergencies. It was a town where everyone's business was out in the air, and it was normal for people to be all up in someone else's space unapologetically. If the community did not like your ongoing romantic relationship, it would become an agenda and point of discussion in the next town meeting, and one would make sure to be there to defend themselves. The community members made sure that they made their stand clear, that they would not get forced to choose sides when the romantic relationship went sideways. If you missed a party, you would get automatically branded and added to the reject list. With all this in mind, it was easy to see why the town was buzzing as everyone grew restless, waiting for their invitations to arrive.

Daniella was about 5 foot tall; melanin beautifully blessed her skin tone, and she could be spotted easily with her rather curvaceous figure. Daniella's family could get described as average, with her father being a man obsessed with farming and her mum blessed with tailoring skills. Together, they managed to provide a decent living for their family ensuring they always had the basic needs. Her parents were Christians who believed in God and were actively involved in church matters. Daniella had three sisters and one brother with whom she shared an unbreakable bond. While growing up, Daniella was famous among her parents- peers, family, and the community for her academic brilliance. A girl who loved reading, but did she?

See, Daniella was not a social butterfly, and of the few friends she had, even she was not so sure they would last long. As a result, Daniella became a bookworm for her to get identified by something, and she had exceptionally excelled at creating this new persona with excellence. What she could not quite understand was how she managed to marvel at her society because people wanted to be associated with her for one reason or another. People saw something in her that she never saw in herself. In fact, throughout her school life, she always ended up being a leader in one way or another. Needless to say, she once won a beauty pageant competition in her senior school. Yes, this writer was not joking when she said Daniella had a striking figure!

For the most part, Daniella spent her life away from her parent's home. Her parents believed that the best education was out of town in a private academy where she would interact with other children from out of the community. No offense to the community, but having been born, studied, and married within the community, they held the opinion that they wanted their children to see what else was out there. They wanted to live through their children, a dream that every parent holds. It had been a hot topic of debate during the town's meetings for months. Still, eventually, the community came to accept and let it slide. Daniella joined boarding school at the early age of eleven years. Throughout her school life, she only spent a few weeks in her parent's home over the school holidays. Most students hated being sent off to boarding school and wanted to stay near their parents, but for Daniella, it was different. She enjoyed being away. She loved the friends she had made while in school. She loved the somewhat equality that came with the uniforms. As the years progressed and Daniella moved on to her senior school and university, she spent less and less time around the community. She officially became branded the town's most educated lady.

The Siblings

Daniella and her siblings shared a strong bond of understanding and love. A bond where they could be at world war with each other, but when a new enemy came, they combined forces and pointed their missiles at the new, now common enemy. Their parents must have been proud of how they had raised them, as was every parent's dream to see their children bonded no matter what. It was common to see siblings kill each other over petty things or siblings with unending rivalry but not this family. They always looked out for each other no matter what, and they had one rule, "We are one team, or you are against the team." A rule that was enforced by their father when they were young. He wanted his family always to present a united front as he knew the benefits of teamwork and unity. Running a cash crop farm as well as a ranch, Daniella's father had employed over ten people. Over the years, he had learned the benefits of encouraging his employees to work together. As a result, he saw his business flourish and wanted to share the same values with his family. It was a simple slogan, yet it helped shape their relationship as they grew up.

Daniella was the last-born child, and having older siblings who had set high standards, she always felt like she needed to do and be more. The eldest was her brother Jack, a hardworking banker, charming with a signature afro hairstyle and a mustache. Jack worked out of town in the big city but preferred to live in the community, so he always drove back and forth each day. Jack had always been the caring big brother who protected his sisters from harm. He was a proud man, as men befriended him so that they could try and get closer to his sisters. Jack was well-liked among the womenfolk as well. Many women wanted to be associated with him. He was branded the most handsome eligible bachelor in the town, and most mothers in the community pointed their daughters in his direction. Moreover, the widows and single mothers also had their eyes on him. He was a hot target as the ladies would discuss him behind closed doors; sometimes, this ended up in catfights. As expected, only one lady would be the lucky one. Jack only had eyes for the past few years for one lady, Daniella's best friend, Rosa.

Rosa and Daniella have been childhood friends. Rosa was from the neighborhood but from a well-off family compared to Daniella's family. She was an only child and about the same height as Daniella. Rosa had grown to be like part of Daniella's family as her parents traveled a lot and often left her under the care of Daniella's parents. Rosa played the piano; her fingers were angelic. Despite being so good at it that it could earn her a decent living in the city doing events, she believed this was not her career calling and considered it merely a hobby. Whenever there was a community event, she volunteered to play the piano for entertainment. She loved being in the spotlight. Rosa was also the town's news editor and was continually updated with the news before it hit the streets.

It was Rosa who had spread the rumors about Daniella's party. She was confident she would be on the guest list, besides nobody leaves out their best friend when they host a party...Right? Daniella wanted both Rosa and her brother to be happy. She, however, believed that Rosa and Jack did not match as a couple. She could not marry the idea of her brother and best friend together!

Her three sisters, Zee, Tora, and Yeli were all unmarried and living their lives. Zee loved painting and art. She had slowly made a name for herself through her paintings and lavish lifestyle. Living near the mountains, Zee bought herself a condo and beautifully furnished it with her paintings and other unique artifacts sourced worldwide. Her backyard was her inspiration and where the magic happened when she did her paintings. Most of which went to charity homes and gifts for her friends. The few she managed to sell went to the highest bidders and spent the money on more charity work. Occasionally she had been invited to display her work in gallery exhibitions, but she had consistently declined, insisting that her artwork was a hobby. Over the years, she had made it clear that her peace of mind was vital to her, and she chose not to involve herself with anything that would jeopardize that. She did not fancy the headache that came with planning for the exhibitions. Zee was also a corporate lady who loved her job. She could run her show by starting her own company, but she preferred to be employed as there was less pressure. Earning over five figures a month, she lived an extraordinary life. With Zee, designer clothes were her type of language, and you would never miss her at lavish parties. Zee was in a long-term relationship, where she and her boyfriend had opted not to commit for reasons best known to them. As the eldest sister, Zee had always been on the lookout for her younger sisters, occasionally assuming the mother figure role.

Tora loved music and was well-known for her dancing skills. Out of them all, she was the party animal. She would party any day and at any time without growing tired. When you think of Ibiza, that was a physical embodiment of Tora. Tora made a living from her business, a nightclub. A business venture that her parents did not readily welcome. Being Christians, they felt this was embarrassing and unbecoming, as it did not represent the values they had instilled in their children. Eventually, they came to accept and support their daughter's venture. The older adults in the community were not happy either, as Tora's nightclub went with a modern touch. It was the new chill zone for the young adults who had slowly started to forget some of the town's traditions, like the weekend baking contest. The nightclub had become so famous that people from outside town would drive up to join in the weekend fun and shenanigans. Her friends from the city loved spending weekends in this part of town. On the brighter side, the venture thrived in the hospitality sector as visitors would need these services. Thus, the elders, the owners of the hotels and restaurants, could not protest for long; this, too, was overlooked.

In this club, most of the town's parties happened, and only Tora would know the guests at any given party. Being the club owner, Tora advised all the event planners who booked the club that having a guest list would make the event more organized. The list would also help the club management optimize the seating layouts and ensure enough food, beverage, and support staff would be available during the party. As a free-spirited person, Tora was never into committed relationships, for she was married to her business and her love for partying. She preferred having friends with benefits instead of any long-term relationship.

Yeli was the rebel of them all, and no one knew what she was good at as she kept changing skills as fast as a chameleon changing colors. She claimed to make a living from traveling and working as an influencer. A concept that most people in the community did not understand. Having studied out of town, Yeli had seemingly picked up on this otherwise foreign trend to the people in her community and had made it her lifestyle. Yeli was a globe trotter, and no one knew where exactly she was at any given time. At the age of twenty-nine, she still lived in her parent's house as she did not see the point of renting or buying her place because she was constantly traveling. On the nights she was in town and partying it up at Tora's club, she opted to spend the nights at Zee's home as she never wanted the parents to see her hungover. Whenever you were idle, you could visit her social pages and keep up with her adventures and jet-set lifestyle.

Yeli was the chatterbox in the family and the family linguistics because she learned languages very easily and quickly. This skill explained why it was easy for her to travel and blend in with the locals of the country she visited. The funny thing was that she always found her way back to the town whenever there was a party. It seemed she was constantly informed of what was happening no matter where she was. Or was it one of the benefits of your sister owning the town's party place? Yeli had claimed to have a boyfriend out of town, but none of the siblings had ever met him nor seen a picture of him. They all assumed he was imaginary and had grown tired of asking about him.

Regardless of how busy life was, the siblings always made time to meet and do what siblings do best-have weird conversations that included gossiping about relatives, neighbors, ex-boyfriends, and ex-girlfriends, among other things. They would also meet to support each other in their careers and business ventures. On other occasions, they had meetings to intervene when one's behaviors had become questionable or worrying.

The Boyfriends

When it came to romantic relationships, sometimes it was love at first sight, and other times it was born out of convenience. Believing herself to be socially awkward, Daniela didn't quite know how to navigate relationships. She was unsure what was supposed to happen. "What were the correct rules of this thing called love? Was there a school where they offered this training?" she often wondered. Compared to her peers, Daniella seemed slightly different. Her intentions regarding relationships had been purely for love and not any other material things. She wanted to have someone in her corner; she needed someone to confide in apart from Rosa. Daniella had never dated anyone from her town as she did not fancy everyone being all up in her business.

She met her first love on a night out with her sister Tora. Tora had a business meeting near Daniella's university and, as was her character, had decided to make it a night out, dragging Daniella along with her. Daniella had tried to dodge Tora with the excuse that she had been swamped with schoolwork. But, knowing her sister would never give up, especially when it came to a night out with family, she had to throw in the towel and accept the invitation. Being a weekend, she figured she had nothing to lose. Looking at the crowd in the club that evening, it was evident that everyone was looking forward to blowing the week's steam. Tora selected a table near the dance floor, and once they had settled, the waitress served tequila shots to get them in the mood as instructed by Tora. As the night progressed, Tora saw an old friend on her way to the bathroom and invited him and his two friends to join them at their table as they had come in late, and the early comers took all tables. Again, the waitress served more tequila shots ordered by Tora's friend, and Daniella decided to loosen up and join the crowd on the dance floor. The DJ was doing a fantastic job as the crowd loved his vibe. However, before Daniella knew it, Timmy, one of the guys at their table, had joined her. He had the sexiest smile Daniella had ever seen. Ooh! How he danced smoothly was like she had seen an angel or, as the soap operas go, her "Alejandro." Daniella did not want the night to end. She was having more fun than she had expected. It was that, or maybe she had drunkenly surmised, had Timmy cast a love spell in the air?

As with all good things, the night ended, and as luck would have it, Timmy asked Daniella for her number. Daniella scribbled it for him on a piece of paper as his phone battery had given up the ghost in dire need of a charge. Daniella herself believed that the guy was the initiator. So, she had wanted to avoid getting his number, knowing she would never make the first call. However, the following day Daniella could not get him off her mind. Thoughts such as "Could one fall in love at first sight? Did he like me back? I am sure he had charmed lots of girls, and there was no way he was single" ran through her mind. "Why had he not called yet?"

As the days passed, she slowly started believing that it had all been in her head until a month later when she received a call from him. Daniella had wanted to scream in excitement as he introduced himself, but she had managed to maintain her calm. As Daniella learned later, Timmy liked her too but had accidentally misplaced the piece of paper with her number from that evening they met. Tora's other friend, who had been present on the night Daniella had met Timmy, and been a closer friend to Tora's, had gone AWOL on work duty to a remote area with no cell phone service. There was no way for Timmy to reach out to him to get Daniella's number from Tora then. Finally, only a month later, he resurfaced from his remote work duty and could get in touch with Tora on his friend's behalf to get the number.

Timmy was free-spirited, wild, and undeniably fun. She loved his vibe and loved being around him. She always looked forward to their dates. They had a favorite spot for their meets; a restaurant in the city close to the club where they had met the first time on the night out with Tora. They both liked the restaurant as it had a great view of the city and local and international food choices. It also had less footfall, giving them privacy to enjoy each other's company. She loved how they would do daring things and enjoyed the adrenaline rush. For the first time in a long time, she felt like he understood her like he not only got her oddness but embraced her quirkiness as well. She was in love, and like most first love stories, they never lasted long, and Daniella was no exception. Unfortunately, two years later, they had to end their relationship as her prince charming had found a new queen for himself. She was deeply heartbroken, as deep down she always thought they would last forever and sail off into happily ever after.

As is the nature of life, it moved on, and the wound she thought would never heal healed with time. However, heartbreak is a cruel teacher whose lessons and scars remain despite time. One gift, first love with Timmy had given her, was trust issues. She, therefore, was not sure if any of the men she met were all in or if they, too, would leave her heartbroken. Consequently, she decided to have her exit plan. Part of her would be entirely in, and the other part would be out and sniffling for new options. Her heart became stone cold with time. She chose to deal with her heartbreak like a failed exam that had no choice for repeats or retakes. For her, it meant changing the entire course. A closed chapter was a closed chapter.

Years later, she met a new prince charming while minding her business in a mall. Frustrated over how the day was unfolding, Daniella was sitting on a bench and watching something on her phone when she heard someone greet her. She looked up, and there was this handsome man with a well-maintained beard and a bald head dressed in navy khaki shorts and a fitting white t-shirt. His masculine physique could not go unnoticed. He had reached out his hand, with a breathtaking smile on his face, and introduced himself as Jacob, asking her what her name was in return. Typically, she would have been rude and ignored him, but on this occasion, it was like there was a spell cast at that exact moment. She stammered as she told him her name. He had sat beside her as they conversed, and her heart pounded faster than an antelope from a chase with the lion. She made a fool of herself by blubbering words that made no sense. "Could he please stop smiling?" Daniella had screamed to herself in her head. They exchanged numbers and, after that, started meeting up for dates.

When with Jacob, Daniella felt like a teenager again. As she learned from Jacob's friend one evening that Jacob had invited her to his friend's birthday party, it was not the first time he had seen her. Jacob had spotted Daniella at least three times on different occasions when she was in the city, and he had convinced himself it was not by chance. As time passed, Daniella discovered he was wild in his way, loved having a good time, and they shared common goals and interests. He loved her in a way she had not felt before. He was gentle with her and respected her opinions. As the years passed, she became fully absorbed this time, opening her heart up again. Three years later into the relationship, Daniella was secretly hoping that this would be her last attempt at this love test. She believed she had gone through her academy of love and had exhausted her phase of trials and errors. She wanted to settle down, build a life, and have her kids. She couldn't help but thank her lucky star when Jacob got down on his knees and proposed to her. It was even way better than she could have imagined it. Every girl wants to see her prince charming on his knees and her dream came true. Guess this prince charming would last happily ever after.

The fact that Daniella was engaged was not lost on the people of the community. Could it be that the party was the wedding in disguise? Is this why there was a guest list?

The Job

From a young age, Daniella had always wanted to run her own show. As her character was not so social, she preferred to observe people from a distance, which opened her up to being a photographer. Daniella had an eye for detail when it came to photography and was flexible and patient in her quest to capture a perfect moment. Her passion for photography made it the ideal career choice for her as she would work with people without having to have long, awkward conversations. For over two years after graduating from the university, she had tried to apply for jobs in reputable companies, but her efforts were futile. In fact, one of her college professors had told her that she was better off doing another course instead of photography. "Was he right?" she sometimes wondered to herself whenever she received a reject email from the jobs she had applied for when searching for jobs. After countless disappointments, she decided to venture out on her own. She was determined not to be a failure in her career. She started by taking photos of the masterpiece paintings that Zee did. She would then post them on her website and her other social platforms. Whenever there was an event, she would take pictures and market herself through them. Her friends and families made referrals, while others became her best retainer clients.

Like any other business, there were ups and downs, but since she loved the job, she was not ready to give up whenever she met an obstacle. Like a small fire spreading over a forest, Daniella slowly penetrated the industry until everyone knew her name in her small town and other major cities. Demand for her work increased, and big brands wanted to work with her. She became like a goddess in the photography industry. With fame came social meetups, as everyone wanted to be associated with her. Five years into the business, Daniella had become more social. She was excited as her dream of everyday social life slowly became a reality. She made many friends to the point that even Rosa would complain that she felt left out. She also made many critics, but that never bothered Daniella, or so she thought.

Other photographers would seek Daniella's opinion as she had inspired many in the industry. Hence, it was a hot topic when rumors spread that she would be hosting a party with a guest list. As the word spread about the party, Daniella started receiving gifts from people trying to buy their way to the guest list.

The Coach and Counselor

With her seemingly overnight success and fame, Daniella felt like she was losing her mind and creativity, so she decided to seek help. She started seeing Mr. Antonio, a life coach, and counselor. A well-polished man who wore expensive watches and had a dimple on his left cheek. He was a handsome young man, unmarried, and most of his patients were women. Yes, he was a good-looking man, and at one point, Daniella had secretly had a crush on him, but she had to stop the madness as she loved her fiancée and wanted to keep things with her coach professional. Mr. Antonio furnished his office with an office desk and chair next to the window. A bookshelf on the opposite wall from the desk. A three and two-seater couch was neatly arranged in the middle and separated by a wooden table. There was also a fireplace on the opposite wall from the door and a giant clock beautifully displayed. Since Mr. Antonio operated from the city, it was easy for Daniella to keep the secret and not have the community all up her business.

There was something about coaches, excellent listeners, astute and attentive, and always asking just the right questions at the right time and with the right tone. Pushing for answers but never demanding them, getting one to lower their guards in ways they would have never otherwise done. When Daniella first visited Mr. Antonio, she was not sure that having a coach would help her. As far as Daniella knew, she believed that what she was experiencing came from fatigue and being burnt out. She had taken a mini vacation to Maldives, where she had hoped to have time to herself and relax. During the holiday, Daniella was proud of herself as she felt she had found the answers she was looking for to regain her creativity. She had done quality reflection on her life and career and had great plans for her business. However, when she came back, everything had returned to how it had been before she had left for her vacation. Her motivation disappeared; she felt like she wanted a lazy day every day. It was during that time that she decided to take up her fiancée's suggestion and seek professional help.

During one of their sessions, they had explored ways in which Daniella could get back to feeling in control and not like she was losing her mind. They had discussed the performance and how she could showcase her work in a way that felt authentic, true, and reflective of her. Daniella opted for an exhibition that an after-party would follow as she saw this was the best way of launching her latest collections. However, she didn't want to get so caught up that she lost herself and her love for her work in the process. She wanted an exhibition that would be true and represent her newly discovered inner peace. Part of her wanted to have everyone on board, but the other part wanted to have a small circle of people with whom she could have intimate conversations. Mr. Antonio asked Daniella what she really desired, and she said she wanted both outcomes. He then gently prompted her to decide, asking her to take a moment and visualize both scenarios. Next, he asked her to look at herself in both scenes and watch her body language and how she felt in each. However, before Daniella could answer, she received an emergency call, and they had to conclude their session earlier than expected. As they finalized the session, Mr. Antonio suggested that Daniella consider holding the exhibition and after-party with a guest list.

Daniella had looked at him dumbfounded. How in God's name did he expect her to do such a thing? The whole town would want, no…expect an invitation. She had told him about her upbringing; he knew where she came from and what she had gone through. He was aware that her friends from out of town would want an invite too. She couldn't have a guest list! Whom would she exclude? Invite? The more she thought and considered Mr. Antonio's suggestion, the more livid she became. She told him that having a guest list was as good as social and career suicide. She went on and on, ranting to her heart's content, throwing every excuse under the sun at him. The whole time, Mr. Antonio took notes and listened with a keen ear while watching her body language and facial expressions. Once she was done talking and had calmed down, he reminded her that it was merely a suggestion and she was not obliged to consider it. Having temporarily forgotten about her emergency, Mr. Antonio asked her to sleep on the idea of having an exhibition and after-party with a guest list as they concluded the session. Walking her out the door, he told her they would resume their discussion at her next appointment.

Daniella could not sleep that night. The idea of having a guest list did not sit well with her. "He must have had bad intentions for me," she thought. "Should I go back to him again or look for a new coach? Ugh! What in God's name sent me to this man? Is he even qualified to run a business?" she had asked herself in frustration.

As she tossed and turned in sleepless worry, she thought of the three years she had seen Mr. Antonio as a coach and how he had always rightly guided her. Despite not understanding him now, she concluded that he must have had his reasons. Besides, he was a certified Neuro-linguistics practitioner and life coach and had a Bachelor of Science in psychology. She quickly decided against changing coaches, and with that decision, she was finally able to fall asleep.

Having been her coach for three years, Mr. Antonio was confident that this suggestion was a masterpiece, as over their sessions, Daniella had always complained after any parties or events she attended. She would go on and on about how a certain person pretended to be her friend. So, he was determined to make his client feel better, and that's why he believed having an exclusive guest list for the exhibit and after-party would help immensely. However, he knew only Daniella could make the final decision and do what she felt was best for her. Besides, in his line of work, his job was to create breakthroughs and hope his clients took the leap.

The Planning

With months to go to the party, Daniella had to make her guest list. While she had the option of involving her best friend Rosa who was dying to jump in and quicken the process of coming up with the guest list and the planning, Daniella knew that she could not involve anyone in this task as only she understood what she wanted to achieve. She had promised Rosa that she would give her the greenlight once her guest list had been ready. She wanted her guests to represent authenticity. She was tired of the fake friends who only used her to get ahead in the industry, tired of faking smiles during conversations she had no interest in participating. She was tired of making public appearances when she could be in the comfort of her own home, binge-watching movies and television shows over a glass or two of her favorite wine. She wanted peace of mind and authenticity. She wanted to be honest and speak her mind when the need arose.

To those around her, Daniella was a woman in control. A woman who had solutions and bucketloads of confidence. Her work and name had spread in major towns and cities like wildfire in a forest within a time scale of five years since she started her venture in photography. People loved her and wanted to be associated with her. Daniella was the woman people would go to for solutions whenever they got stuck and needed more insights regarding photography. She was a smart one when it came to making a living.

While things were taking shape in her quest for social excellence in her adult life, Daniella was inwardly suffering from a childhood nightmare that made no sense to her. Her parents had taken her to church every Sunday when she was younger and still living with them. Each time this nightmare occurred; she would question the existence of God. Daniella felt uncomfortable opening up to those in her inner circle that she struggled with a nightmare. The one time she had opened up about her nightmare was to Rosa, who had dismissed her worries and fears, telling her it was merely a dream.

With all this, it had been evident that Daniella had a tough time getting the guest list ready and planning for the invite-only party. Whom could she invite? Whom could she not invite? Would the list affect her career? Would the list affect her social life?

The Nightmare

The nightmare had come up during her one session with Mr. Antonio. They had been delving into her childhood, and she had been explaining how she thought it had negatively affected her adulthood. "Tell me more about this nightmare," Mr. Antonio had prodded gently. He had skillfully driven the conversation to this point, but he had done it in such a way that made Daniella feel safe to share and open up and in a way that had made her feel like this had been her idea. Pausing briefly, she took a deep breath before responding,

"Each time, the same nightmare came to me. I kept screaming for help, but my voice could not be heard. I could not even hear myself scream in my head. I would run for miles but felt like I was not moving forward or fast enough. The monster would laugh at me, at my lack of strength and willpower, " At this moment, there was an outburst of tears. She continued, "I would throw a punch and still not hit my target H-E-L-P! H-E-L-P! H-E-L-P! I would say, gasping for air. I would wake up sweaty with my bedding wet. My sister, with whom we shared the room at that time, used to assume I had wet the bed." she concluded, taking a deep breath and reaching out for the tissues on the table to wipe her tears.

Mr. Antonio was keen to understand and hear more of this nightmare as, from a coaching perspective, he knew that people often tended to distort or misinterpret reality. Further, he knew that human beings were inclined to selectively pay attention to specific aspects of an experience and overlook the others. He believed that knowledge, memories, and imaginations were the results of sequences and combinations in which the information got filtered by the human brain and stored. Therefore, he asked Daniella to think about that childhood nightmare as she prepared her guestlist. He believed it was from this nightmare that she would understand what she was running away from and what she was looking for to get the peace of mind she wanted.

Mr. Antonio explained to Daniella that from his reading adventures, he had discovered that dreaming was part of a thinking process. It was a continuation of the day's thoughts that continued as one drifted off to sleep and entered the Rapid Eye Movement (REM) cycle of sleep. The thoughts continued in the form of symbols instead of actual words. During REM sleep, some parts of the brain that control rational thoughts are dormant. In contrast, other parts that control emotions become highly active, and one could consider them a metaphoric exposition of oneself. However, he cautioned Daniella that these were just studies conducted. As the world evolved with technological advancements, more theories would be coming.

Mr. Antonio, moreover, believed that the nightmare was born from Daniella's fears. What she had fed her subconscious mind translated into and came alive in her nightmare. From his study of the human brain when pursuing his undergraduate in psychology, he believed that nightmares resulted from electrical thoughts pulled from one's memories. Thus, he was determined to help Daniella see that the nightmare held no basis for who she was and what her future self would become.

Listening to Mr. Antonio share his knowledge, Daniella had mixed feelings and thoughts running through her mind. Part of her had been excited and thrilled that there was hope and that she would better understand her nightmare. She could not believe that there had been a possible explanation behind her nightmare. The other part of her was unsure that she was ready to unveil the reasons behind her nightmare. However, by the end of her conversation with Mr. Antonio, she had been convinced that she was ready to find meaning in her nightmare.

The Monster

Mr. Antonio walked Daniella through the nightmare. He believed each part of the nightmare held a significant meaning. Each time he asked her to lie on the three-seater couch in his office, close her eyes and go back to the nightmare, he focused on one part to not overwhelm her. The first part was the monster.

"Can you identify what or do you know why or whom you are screaming at?" Mr. Antonio asked her.

"Yes," she replied hesitantly, "at the monster."

"And what makes you say it's a monster?" he asked.

"Well, because it's ugly and hideous," Daniella resorted almost fearfully. She was sinking back into the couch almost as if trying to make herself as small and invisible as possible. Mr. Antonio noted this and asked gently, trying to draw her further into her nightmare so they could explore the monster further before she could work herself into a frenzy.

"Is there something the monster is doing or has done to you to cause you to feel unsafe?" he asked.

Daniella seemed unsure for a second but responded quietly, "He is terrifying to look at, and he is running after me and keeps laughing out in a horrid loud voice."

"Apart from how he appears or looks and the horrid laughter, does the monster attempt to speak to you or try to communicate with you?" he asked.

"I don't know, I just want to get away from him," she replied.

Mr. Antonio noted that Daniella was a lot calmer than she had been when they first began talking about the monster when he asked her to return to her nightmare memory. Nevertheless, he decided to continue with his line of questioning, hoping to get her to move past her fear of the monster.

"Did the monster attempt to hurt you at any time?" he asked.

Daniella frowned as she thought about the question. It took some time before she responded with a "No."

Mr. Antonio decided to change the line of questioning and instead asked Daniella to describe what she could see in her nightmare.

After a while, Daniella responded, "I see a huge thing with the same features as a normal human. However, I see that he is green in color and his feet and hands are bigger than the average human size. I feel terrified to be in the same environment as him."

"I want you to pay close attention and look at the monster Daniella," said Mr. Antonio, closely watching her, "What made you say the monster is laughing at you?" At this moment, Daniella was shaking her head in dismay, and her fists clenched tightly. Then, noticing the change, Mr. Antonio had asked her to take slow deep breaths, and seeing her ease, he had proceeded, "I need you to look at him and tell me if the monster is laughing at you or being friendly."

"I don't know," Daniella said, vehemently shaking her head, "And I cannot turn back to look at him."

Mr. Antonio was sensing Daniella's unease mounting, and he had asked her to open her eyes. Next, he asked her to describe how she felt as he could see she seemed low. Daniella had taken some water before she confessed that she felt like a trapped teenager again and did not like the feeling at all. At this point, Mr. Antonio asked her to take a five-minute break to get some fresh air, change scenery, and gather her thoughts. After the break, Mr. Antonio asked Daniella to close her eyes again, except this time round, she would watch herself in the nightmare as a bystander. Noticing Daniella's reluctance, Mr. Antonio had asked her to take three deep breaths and nod whenever she was ready for them to continue with the session. After a minute of silence, Daniella nodded, and Mr. Antonio continued with his line of questioning.

"As a bystander, how would you describe the scene?" he asked.

There was a minute of pin-drop silence before Daniella responded. "I see two main characters. One seems to be a male character wearing dark brown checked trousers with a tattered white sleeveless shirt and has no shoes on. The other character is a young girl about the age of eight years. The girl is wearing a sky-blue jogger set with white sneakers. She also has her hair plaited in cornrows hairstyle." There was another minute of silence before Daniella continued, "The girl seems terrified of the other character, who appears to be happy with their ongoing activity. They are running in circles after each other. Despite the girls' expressions of fear, the scene is comedic in a way, with the way they are running in circles, almost like a dog chasing its tail, except it's hard to know who is chasing or chased." She concluded with a smile on her face as if enjoying the view. Noticing the smile on Daniella's face, Mr. Antonio allowed her to live that moment for about one minute as he scribbled some notes on his notepad before he double-checked with her whether she had missed out on any details from the scene. After which, Daniella responded with a "No" cheerfully.

Without any delay, Mr. Antonio asked Daniella to open her eyes and asked her how she had felt while observing that part of her nightmare as a bystander. Consequently, Daniella explained that she felt confused as, for the longest time, she knew and believed that there was something or someone after her. With that revelation, Mr. Antonio asked Daniella to close her eyes, return to the nightmare, and relieve it once more. He asked her to utilize the knowledge she had acquired as a bystander. At that very minute, Daniella excused herself to use the bathroom. Once she was back and settled on the couch with her eyes closed, Mr. Antonio asked her to describe the nightmare again without leaving out any details. After a while, Daniella said, "I am in the countryside and running after something, or something is running after me. It is not very clear. I feel terrified and angry. But I also sense fear wallowing within me. I want to stand and face what is behind me but am scared to turn, so I keep running," in a subdued voice.

At this juncture, Mr. Antonio asked gently, "With the knowledge, we have gained in the last couple of minutes, I want you to observe your surroundings carefully and tell me what is causing the feelings of fear."

There was silence for about forty seconds, "I am not sure; the countryside looks so peaceful. However, I have this feeling deep down in my heart that keeps telling me to run. It is the same feeling I get whenever I meet new people" she replied with an intense voice. Noticing the shift in her facial expression where she looked worried and the intense voice, Mr. Antonio asked her to take some deep breaths before he continued to probe her gently with the questions.

"What else can you tell me about this feeling?" he had asked.

After some time, Daniella replied, "I don't know how to explain it, but I have always equated the feeling with it being my savior as I know it protects me from harmful situations."

Mr. Antonio noticed Daniella's voice was lower, and he decided to continue questioning to understand more of what she had meant. "You have mentioned that you have always equated that feeling to being your savior. What gave you that impression? Could you give me an example, please?" he asked.

"Well," Daniella had started to respond, then paused as if carefully deciding which example to give; then she continued, "when I was about eleven years old, my school had organized a science fair competition. As one of the brightest students, the teachers thought I was the best candidate to represent the school in the competition. At first, I was excited that I would get to make a presentation in front of a large crowd and to students from different schools. I planned to make my school proud and envisioned myself receiving the winning trophy. With the support of my teachers, friends, and classmates, I prepared a masterpiece that they all agreed would bring the trophy home. However, toward the competition date, I started developing cold feet. Whenever I envisioned the competition, all I could see were people laughing at me during my presentation. I also saw my teachers telling me how much of a failure I was because I did not bring the trophy home. A week before the presentation, the panic got worse, and all I could hear was a voice telling me to run.

And so, I listened, and three days into the competition, I faked an illness, and luckily the school nurse confirmed that I was sick. One of my team members had to step in, as being the organizers of the event and the hosting school, it would not be wise for us not to have a presentation. The truth is things went exactly as I had envisioned; the only difference is that I was not the one doing the presentation. I am grateful to that warning voice that told me to run, which saved me from embarrassment and ridicule. I further, had maintained my social status in school."

Mr. Antonio considered what he was hearing before finally responding, "Wow, that is a power-packed and interesting story. So now I do get some insight into where you are coming from with the inner voice you mentioned earlier. Have you ever considered that the events on that particular day occurred that way since the main presenter, who was you, developed cold feet and the student who stepped in was not prepared psychologically for that role?" he had asked.

Swiftly Daniella responded with a "No" followed by "I have never looked at it from that perspective before," and seemed deep in thought.

Giving her time to digest the information, Mr. Antonio sipped from his cup of coffee. Then he continued, "Have you also ever considered that maybe if you had done the presentation, things might have turned out differently?"

Daniella shrugged her shoulder but, shaking her head, she had said skeptically, "I honestly doubt that." At which point Mr. Antonio replied,

"That's all right; now I want you to open your eyes and come back to the present moment," he had said while scribbling some notes on his notepad. Once Daniella had settled sitting up, he continued, "From what I have heard from you; I could brand the inner voice that tells you to run as your defense mechanism. Just like the wood frog creates its natural antifreeze to avoid being frozen alive, you avoid situations that you think may affect your social status."

At this point, Daniella had stood up and walked to the window in Mr. Antonio's office. Then, she responded, "Not sure I would call it a defense mechanism, but that's just about right. It saves me a lot of heartache." It was raining cats and dogs, and Mr. Antonio noticed that his client seemed fascinated with the view. Allowing her to live in that moment, he had excused himself to use the bathroom. When he returned, Daniella had settled back seated on the couch and ready to continue.

"Let us start from your last comment," he had said. "I hear you, Daniella, and I have understood from the example you gave me what led you to that conclusion, which leads to my next question. What do you really fear in your everyday life today?" he had asked.

"Hmmm!... I don't know!" Daniella had said thoughtfully and paused as if trying to remember something, "Don't we all have something we are afraid of?" she then asked.

"You are right, Daniella," Mr. Antonio said with a smile. "There are some things we are all afraid of and have no control over, such as death. But I want you to move past that and think. What is the one thing that scares you the most?" he had asked.

Daniella had seemed to be lost in thoughts staring at the oversized wall clock in Mr. Antonio's office, "I guess I was afraid of being rejected when I was young. But as an adult, I am sure that's not the case now." she said thoughtfully.

"What makes you say that?" Mr. Antonio asked.

"Have you seen my circle of friends? I am a superstar out here." Daniella said as she chuckled.

"Yes, I have seen your following on social media and all the great and kind words people write to you, but I want us to go beyond the surface and dig a little deeper. In your earlier statement, you mentioned that as a child, you feared rejection. Could you share an instance showing you experienced rejection as a child?" Mr. Antonio asked.

Taking a sip from her cup of English tea that Mr. Antonio's assistant had prepared for her, Daniella said, "If I am going, to be honest, I cannot recall any instance that I received a rejection." Seemingly enjoying her beverage.

"Tell me, Daniella, are you cautious when letting people in?" Mr. Antonio asked.

Taking another sip from her cup of English tea, "Uhm-yes, no, maybe…" she had responded.

"Do you sometimes have difficulty trusting people with your feelings?" Mr. Antonio asked.

She put her cup of tea on the table, "That is a big yes!" she said with a smile.

"Do you sometimes find yourself doing things to please others?" Mr. Antonio had asked.

"Well, using my definition of pleasing others, I would say Maybe." she had replied as she chuckled.

"Do you easily make negative assumptions about what others are thinking?" Mr. Antonio had asked.

Enjoying this line of questioning, "Half the time…." Daniella responded with a giggle.

There was a slight pause as Mr. Antonio seemed to be cross-checking his notes. Then, he continued, "Looking at the answers you have given me, do you think you have already implanted rejection even before you have lived it or faced it?" He had asked.

There was a moment of silence as Daniella reflected on how she had made bad choices to please her friends. She clearly remembered how, when in university in her second year, she had finally got the attention of two third-year students whom most of the students wanted to impress and be associated with for their lavish lifestyle. On one Wednesday afternoon, they invited Daniella to join them in the city for a shopping spree for an upcoming end-year party at the university. Despite having a lecture scheduled that afternoon, Daniella opted to skip the class and join her newly formed friends as she wanted to be kept in the friendship circle. Daniella had not known that it would be her first day dealing with the police. As bad luck would have it, while Daniella was busy trying on sunglasses in one high-end store they had visited, her friends were busy hiding sets of earrings and bracelets in Daniella's bag. The metal detector started to beep as they walked out of the store. As with the procedure, carefully checking their bags with the security staff, and to Daniella's disbelief, there was a reason for the door detector beeping. In shock, Daniella denied that she had taken the items, and the scene had started to cause chaos. Her friends had left her, and since only the store manager had access to the camera footage and had been away for a meeting, the store staff decided to call the police to handle the matter. The police had taken Daniella to the station and locked her up while waiting for the footage to be retrieved.

Luckily for her, the footage worked in her favor and had been released, with the officers advising her to stay away from such friends. However, while it had been such a relief, she still had spent some hours in jail. On other occasions, she said Yes to things when she knew she wanted to say No, like when she had lost her virginity to a man she barely knew. Having joined the university, Daniella had experienced pressure left and right as she was the only one in her group of friends who had never had sexual intercourse. Whenever her friends talked about men, they would mock her for her lack of experience, and Daniella decided enough was enough. But then, it had been one evening at a house party when John, a student trying to get Daniella's attention, invited her to go upstairs for some private talk. Daniella could not explain how the events unfolded after she went upstairs. All she remembered was that deep down in her heart, she clearly did not want to have sexual intercourse with John but had let herself go in the moment to fit in with her friends. At another time, she had stayed in a toxic relationship to avoid the heart turmoil bound to follow a breakup. Then on the flip side, she had ended good relationships out of fear that the day would finally come and the man would decide it was over.

"Oh, My God! How in God's name did I end up here?" Daniella had exclaimed as the proverbial penny had dropped. Mr. Antonio had gone on to explain to Daniella that the monster in her nightmare was symbolic, as it symbolized her greatest fear. He had further explained to her that her fear of rejection came from her believing she was not good enough.

"I am advancing my studies in psychology, and part of my research work delves into the impact of our surroundings," he stated, "as human beings evolve, they tend to pick up things from their surroundings or experiences. For instance, if adults frequently tell a child they are not good enough, these thoughts slowly become part of the child's subconscious mind. With time they manifest themselves in many forms such as dreams, eventually becoming their reality." He further explained to her that in his opinion and experience, he had believed and observed that in the current era, many people end up not pursuing their passions where their strengths were simply because of the words spoken. For example, you may have heard stories from people saying they did not pursue a particular line of work because someone they believed in had told them they did not fit in line with that job. As a result, they ended up in a different industry and were unhappy.

Daniella was puzzled and simultaneously stunned by how Mr. Antonio was helping her connect the dots. However, her mind was still stuck on the science competition, and she wondered how her childhood surroundings contributed.

"From our conversations," Mr. Antonio had continued putting his writing pad on the wooden table, "I have picked up that you were a bright student. I am curious to know one thing, what was the reward system from both your teachers and parents?" he had asked.

"Funny you would ask that," Daniella chuckled, then she responded, "Where I come from, if you never scored 100%, then there was a problem. I remember one time I missed the mark by 1%, and I was proud to take my results home. I still remember my father's question asking me what had happened to the 1% and that conversation had ended there. That had caught me off-guard and left me miserable. In my head, I was expecting a reward and hoped my father would be proud of me, his daughter. That evening I refused to eat my dinner and went to bed early to cry before my sister joined me. I felt like my father had rejected me."

After she had finished speaking and had some thoughtful silence, Mr. Antonio asked her, "What happened after that evening? What thoughts always come to you whenever you face something that looks like a test?"

"Well, to be honest," Daniella had started to respond before she took a sudden pause and seemed to be lost in thoughts, "Most of the time, I get scared that I may give my best and still get rejected. I vividly have that scenario with my father in my head." she continued. After that response, an awkward silence transpired. It seemed Daniella had found her answer. She had developed cold feet before the competition as she had feared the reaction that would have followed if she had not succeeded and come out on top.

Mr. Antonio had asked Daniella to go down memory lane again and, this time round, think of the things that had troubled her growing up. Daniella remembered occasions when she was uncomfortable with her beautiful skin tone; many people around her were light-skinned, including her siblings. They commented on how they wouldn't dream of having a different melanin skin tone. When she was about fourteen years old, she believed she was cursed and felt like she did not fit in because boys seemed to prefer light-skinned girls, which reduced her self-esteem. Studying in a boarding school, her classmates and friends would receive letters from boys in neighboring schools but not Daniella. To everyone, she had painted a picture that she had no interest in boys and wanted to concentrate on her books, but deep down; she was unsparing of self-criticism. Some of her peers tried to change their skin tone by bleaching. Still, deep down, Daniella knew nothing was wrong with her skin color as she had learned from Sunday School that all human beings were beautiful and fearful, made in the image and likeness of God. Still, the outside pressure had surpassed that truth.

She remembered how her body shape had bothered her as well. Daniella had tried to starve herself on several occasions to shed some weight as she had received comments that she ate more than her portion but that never worked. Whenever there were family functions, she would find an excuse not to attend, as it was there that a significant part of her body shaming occurred. It was a regular and funny conversation with her relatives as they believed they were right. As their cultural beliefs went, a young lady should have a slim body. These comments offended Daniella, as how her body look was beyond her. From the day Daniella was born, she had been a chubby baby. As she grew up, her body formed excellent hips and curves, a trait she had inherited from her mother. She remembered how her love for books made her less popular with the cool kids, "show off," they would always whisper when she was around.

There had been a brief moment of silence before Mr. Antonio explained to Daniella that the monster could symbolize all the instances she had mentioned. He further explained that, as she grew older, her subconscious mind kept believing that she would be rejected or ridiculed. Thus, as a defense mechanism, she would reject people before they first rejected her. At this point, Daniella seemed to agree with Mr. Antonio and had been nodding her head all through.

Daniella had built a name for herself by becoming the best in the industry. The career was noble, but she realized her intentions had not been. She had to face the fact that she wanted to be worshiped and punish all those who rejected her or made her feel rejected. She had achieved her goal, as everyone wanted to be associated with her. However, the question remained, why was she still not happy?

As the session ended, Mr. Antonio gave Daniella a task. He asked her to create her first draft of her supposed guest list, keeping in mind the monster in her dreams and what it symbolized. He instructed her to think of the people she had rejected for whatsoever reason, to think of people she had wanted to be associated with once upon a time but, for one reason or the other, had lost connection with along the way due to fears. Daniella had been aware that this meant she would have to get down her guard and get to work. Mr. Antonio had instructed her that she would list down the names under three categories:

The first is Familial Rejection:

In this category, she would look at her nuclear and extended family members and think of those with whom she had lost touch. She would ask herself why that alienation had happened and if she would like to reconcile with them and save the relationship. Daniella had a few family members that had made her feel awful growing up, and she had cut ties with them. The reason had been that they had made insensitive callous comments about her body. She had to choose whether or not she wanted to be reassociated with them again, as they were family, after all.

The second Social Rejection:

Social rejection was familiar to Daniella. She knew she was struggling socially before but had not understood the reasons why. The school was her happy place, and when she reflected, she could not recall any instance she had received bullying or alienation. She then realized the main problem had been within her arm's reach. It had been around her family that she had felt like she had not been doing enough. Unfortunately, this had translated into her feeling rejected. Daniella had many friends from school whom she had lost contact with because of her insecurities. Some had attempted to keep in touch with her, but her lack of effort in return discouraged them; they had to give up eventually. Rosa had lasted longer as she had come to understand her friend's character and had a thing for her brother Jack. In this category, Daniella had to list down all the people she felt had good intentions and genuinely wanted to be her friend because of her personality and not because of her recently acquired fame in the industry. She would further filter her current friend list and only list down the friendships she would want to maintain. Besides, one cannot be for everyone.

The third and final category would be Romantic Rejection:

Daniella believed she was in a good place with her fiancée; however, Mr. Antonio had asked her to assess herself and ensure she had been all in. Mr. Antonio knew she had a good thing going on but had wanted her to make sure she was getting married for the right reasons she had stated before. In one of their sessions, Daniella had told Mr. Antonio that she believed marriage was about love, respect, companionship, and a deep level of understanding for one another. Mr. Antonio asked Daniella to list the men she had dated before and clearly state why they had broken up. He had hoped that by going through this process, she would be able to pick up a pattern of how she dealt with romantic connections. Daniella had smiled to herself as she thought of how easy she was going to get through this category.

After their session, Daniella felt exhausted and decided to go to bed early that evening after canceling her dinner date with her brother feigning illness. She feared that she would not be able to have a proper conversation with him following the session she had had with her coach. She had wanted to be alone and take some time to think as she had still been perplexed by the revelation of things. The following day she had then decided to leave town and booked herself a hotel in a nearby city where she would be alone to reflect on her sessions with her coach as she listed her supposed list.

Mr. Antonio had further instructed Daniella to only go back for the next session when she had completed her first list, as he had believed that exercise would have helped her reflect and digest the information they had discussed. It had taken Daniella four days away from town to come up with a list of 100 people. Her hotel room had been left a mess, with crumbled pieces of paper strewn around, but she had been happy that her mission had been successful and had tipped the room service heavily as she had left.

Mr. Antonio had looked over the list and had proceeded to ask why she had selected those particular people. In response, Daniella had said it was because they had represented people that she had shut out of her life because of her fears of rejection. The list had represented people who had genuinely meant well to her. She had now wanted to extend an invitation to them, as an olive branch and as a way to try and remedy and try to make up for her actions. She hoped to re-acquaintance herself with them.

As a further explanation, she said, "The truth is, Mr. Antonio, I have lived in a box that has restricted me from exploring many opportunities simply because I am always worrying about what other people will think about what I do or say. I have been a people pleaser and have made bad choices just to fit in. I have lost opportunities just because I didn't want to lose a certain group of friends. I have set goals that are still in writing or in my head because I'm too afraid to step out of my comfort zone. I am afraid of the outcome of any venture I decide to take, constantly thinking about what people would say. A constant thought in my head, and it lingers in my mind. I want to stop the awful habits such as lying and failing to say no to things I dislike or disagree with that I have picked along the way but am too afraid of. I don't want "them" to speak ill of me. I want their approval."

Mr. Antonio had taken a few minutes to reflect on Daniella's speech. He had said, "It takes courage and forgiving oneself to start living the true self. It does not matter what they think or say; what matters is what you say about yourself. Our subconscious mind picks up on things; the more negative we get; the more negativity becomes a reality. Think of your mind as a garden; weeds will grow and take over if you plant flowers but neglect your garden. Our success lies in the filters we have set up in our minds. From my experience, it starts with the little things we do. Things like the words we speak to ourselves. Our mindsets are powerful, Daniella, and we can improve our lives by changing our thoughts. Instead of seeing the negative in something, start feeding your thoughts with positive things. A moment of failure does not have to define you; you can translate it into a lesson. Always remember that people's opinions do not have to become your reality. Rather what you say about yourself is the real deal. If you look at yourself in the mirror and utter or think negative things, and vice versa, they, in turn, have the power to become self-fulfilling prophecies."

To further drive this point to her, he told her of a former client who had visited the United Arab Emirates. He told her how she had purchased a bright blue unicorn outfit and worn it in public places. She had taken videos of herself on the beach, in trains, and in crowded areas and uploaded them on her social platforms. He explained to Daniella that though the children were fascinated and excited to see her, most adults had gone about their business.

Mr. Antonio had wanted her to become and embrace a more authentic version of herself. He had hoped to get her there by getting her to deal with people with whom she had made a genuine connection, which could help her be a better version of herself and help her grow; not just people who made her feel great about herself, but people who also challenged her with positive intentions. In addition, he had decided to explain to her a process called anchoring. He had explained to her that anchoring was a process where one used an external stimulus or event to trigger a specific internal experience. He further explained to her that just like the ship anchor prevents the ship from drifting due to strong winds or currents, an anchor would help her change unwanted feelings to resourceful or positive ones. As an example, he had therefore asked her to recall a relationship in her life in which she had been her most authentic and had no hidden agendas. He had wanted her to remember such a relationship in which she had been truly happy and could honestly admit as much to herself. He had asked her to do so, so that he could ask her to relive those moments and remember all emotions she had experienced then. He had aimed to ask her to use that relationship as her anchor by choosing an anchor device that involved touch. He had instructed her to select an anchor she wouldn't otherwise do in her daily routine, like touching her thumb and forefinger together. By doing so, she would replace the feelings of fear and rejection that would have tried to consume her with positive emotions of happiness and joy whenever she pursued new relationships.

The Screaming

Daniella had been excited and curious to proceed with the sessions, following the interpretation of the monster and what it had symbolized. So, for their next session, Mr. Antonio asked her which part of the dream she wanted to discuss. In response, Daniella said she was more interested in figuring out more of the screams and what they could have symbolized. Mr. Antonio smiled with a nod as he reached out for his notebook. After making sure they were both comfortable and ready to begin the session, he said to her, "If I recall correctly, in the session in which you told me of your nightmare, you said that you were screaming because of the monster." As Daniella nodded in affirmation, he asked her, "Could you tell me how your screaming and there being no sound made you feel?"

Daniella had looked down, and it had taken her a minute before she answered, "I felt awful. I felt like I was worthless, and no one cared about me. I felt like people had decided to look the other way and let the monster have me" she had said.

"But when you described your dream to me, it was just you and the monster in the countryside. Whom did you expect would have heard your screams?' Mr. Antonio had asked.

Daniella went silent for about five minutes before finally answering with a slightly resigned shrug, "I don't honestly know."

"If you don't mind me asking," Mr. Antonio had continued, "You had mentioned that the screams were soundless, so who could you blame for not hearing a soundless scream?" he had asked.

Daniella had become pensive before she had finally responded with furrowed eyebrows, "I..," she had stopped and stared at Mr. Antonio in disbelief before she took a sip from her glass of water. This time, it had been Mr. Antonio's turn to nod in quiet understanding. Then, he decided to change tactics and asked her to consider the names she had included in her guest list. Next, he asked her to lie on the couch and close her eyes to concentrate. Then, she would go back to her nightmare and observe her surroundings to check if she would see any familiar faces. There had been silence in the office for about two minutes as he had patiently waited for her response.

"I am in the countryside, and I see…," Daniella had stopped with her response and had instead opened her eyes and looked at Mr. Antonio. She looked troubled, and when she spoke, she told him that she must have been unobservant in her nightmare. Those people had been there and wanted to help her all along. Still, because of her fear of rejection, she had been oblivious to her environment. She had faced the situation on her own. She had only seen as far as her eyesight could and never thought of what was beyond them.

"I hear you, Daniella," Mr. Antonio had continued with the conversation, "I once read an article that explained that human beings tend to have eyesight that one could describe as judging by what one's eyes saw and the mindsight that depended on how one interpreted a situation. Therefore, how one interprets a situation plays a key role in how one conducts themselves and their behavior. You see, Daniella, when I was taking my coaching training, I learned of a concept called Neuro-Linguistic Programming (NLP) communication model, which shows a pattern in which one receives external information or an event that goes through the five senses, which are how we see, hear, feel, smell or taste things."

"Wow!" Daniella interjected, seemingly intrigued with what her coach was talking about, "that seems to be much information one takes in?" she had asked in curiosity.

"Yes, you are right." Mr. Antonio responded, "That is much information that goes through our senses from external sources or events, which is then filtered where one either deletes certain information by way of selectively paying attention to some information and overlook others, distorts other information by way of misinterpreting reality and making shifts in the experiences of sensory data or finally generalizes that information by making decisions or conclusions based on a set of attitudes. Once complete, one can process small chunks of information, which become their internal representation of that external event. That becomes the awareness state of that person. In return, it influences how their body functions which ultimately translates into their behavior patterns." he paused, noticing Daniella seemed to have a question.

"That sounds like a complex theory, but how does that relate to my situation?" she had asked.

"In your case, you may have deleted the existence of people around you and are ready to help. Thus, in your mind's eye, there was nobody else in your dream, just the two of you." Mr. Antonio had responded. He further explained to her that according to research work by some scientists, several reasons and factors may have led to one having nightmares, including fear, frustration, anger, and helplessness.

Mr. Antonio had explained to Daniella that, in his opinion, he had believed that the spotlight had been on fear in Daniella's case. Her fear of rejection had slowly developed self-esteem issues that had become part of her reality growing up. She could express her fear through the screams, and the nightmare would repeat itself as her communication had been pointless, as she had believed no one had heard her. Instead, she had been screaming, trying to address the fear. Mr. Antonio took a sip from his glass of water as if buying some time for Daniella to absorb what he had said before he asked her, "What are your thoughts about this?"

"You could be right," she had said gently. "Now that you have mentioned it, as an adult, I rarely shed a tear, no matter how painful a situation is. In fact, to the best of my memory, the only time I shed tears is when I cut onions when making a delicious meal." She said while twisting her engagement ring before she looked down at it and said, "and that one time when Jacob proposed to me. I still remember it like it was yesterday," she said joyfully.

After their session had come to an end for the day, Mr. Antonio gave Daniella a task. He had asked her to think of the times she had felt bitter and had suppressed feelings of anger, frustration, pain, and loss. He had asked her to take some time and allow herself to feel the grief for the loved ones she had passed on and lost over the years. He had encouraged her to cry loudly if she had to experience pain, anger, frustrations, and bitterness fully. He had further reminded her that it was okay not to be okay, just as it was not healthy to go on the pretense that all was well and good when deep down, she was overwhelmed, high-strung, and needed a form of release. He'd hoped that by giving her this task, the exercise would help her acknowledge her pain and her past, thereby creating an awareness of their existence and, after that, letting them go. Daniella would also remind herself she was as human as any other person.

Daniella had seriously doubted the success of such a task. She had told Mr. Antonio just as much, even as she had chuckled and humorlessly told him that it would be like a mission impossible as she doubted; she even had any tears left in her. Mr. Antonio chuckled at the imagery she had painted and told her that the whole point was for her to try it and take the leap of faith. He had bid her goodbye and told her he looked forward to their next session. Daniella had driven home deep in thought and, being the doubting Thomas she was, wondered how to accomplish the task ahead of her.

That evening, Daniella and her siblings were to have a sibling dinner date. She had decided to turn up instead of giving an excuse and canceling on them, fearing they would have grown suspicious and concerned about her. So, she had showed up about 30 minutes late, dressed in a dark blue bodycon dress and leather-heeled sandals, and had no make-up. It was clear that Daniella didn't want to be there from how she presented herself, and her sister Tora had made a remark and told her that she looked moody. In response, Daniella chuckled and mumbled, "You have no idea."

Daniella had noticed that there had been a difference in the air that evening. She had looked at her siblings one by one as they conversed. Jack was dressed in a white button-down shirt, with few buttons open to show his physique, khaki trousers, and loafer shoes. Zee, the designer woman, was dressed in an asymmetry sleeve pure white color jumpsuit with wedge shoes that Yeli had bought for her last Christmas. Tora wore a black satin wrap dress with a long slit on the side and chunky heels. And finally, Yeli, the wanderer woman, was dressed in a short denim skirt, knee length boots matched with a leather jacket.

As the evening progressed, Daniella found herself lost in thoughts. Observing her siblings having a lively conversation, Daniella could not help but wonder whether any of her siblings had challenges as she did. She, however, could not help but go against the thought as she believed her siblings had always been open with their lives and had shared the challenges they had experienced. The thoughts continued until later, after having their dinner and making silly jokes, Jack said that he had an announcement to make. He had been excited that he would soon exit the bachelor's squad and join the married gang. He had proposed to Rosa, and she had agreed to marry him.

Daniella gasped, then blurted out, "Oh God!" before she could stop herself as she stared at him blankly.

"Daniella, I wanted to meet you the other day to get your blessings as you and Rosa are best friends. Rosa is scared that she may lose your friendship, but I assured her you love us both and want us to be happy." Jack had explained as he had directly addressed her.

The siblings all stared at Daniella, waiting for her response. There had been a few seconds of awkward silence before Daniella attempted to speak. "Jack….I….," Daniella had said in a quivering voice before bursting into tears. That moment was confusing to everyone as the siblings had never seen Daniella in tears in a very long time. Were they tears of joy or sadness? The siblings had looked bewildered, and it had been obvious they were not sure what to do. Seated next to Daniella, Zee stretched her hand, offered Daniella some tissues, and tapped her slowly on the back.

After a couple of minutes, Daniella stopped sobbing. It seemed Zee's tap had helped to soothe her. As if realizing her surroundings, Daniella shifted her glance around the room as she used the tissues Zee had given her to wipe the tears. "Damn you, Mr. Antonio!" she had mumbled to herself. He must have gotten into her head.

Noticing Daniella had eased down, Jack asked with a concerned voice, "Did I upset you with what I said? Do you not approve of Rosa?"

"Not at all, big brother. If anything, I am happy that you and Rosa found love and happiness in each other. I am glad that Rosa will officially become part of the family." So, Daniella had said and realized that she had appeared emotional that evening. Maybe the sessions with her coach took a toll on her, and her emotions frayed.

"I am relieved to hear that you are happy for both of us, but tell us what is troubling you, baby sister? Are you having issues with Jacob?" Jack had asked.

"Not at all; we are actually in a very good place. The thing is….," Daniella had started to stammer, realizing she was letting the cat out of the box. "I have been seeing someone for the past three years," and before she could finish her statement, Zee interjected in surprise, "Are you cheating on Jacob?" Daniella chuckled as she realized she had used the wrong word to describe her relationship with Mr. Antonio. Daniella finally told her siblings that she had been seeing a counselor who also happens to be a life coach. That day's session had been emotional, hence the tears.

"Wait, Daniella! For three years, did anybody else know about this? Is everything all right? "Tora had asked, staring blankly at her other siblings. Embarrassed that her siblings had found out her secret, Daniella's first instinct had been to put up her defense. But then, thoughts and panic had run rampant in her mind as she had wondered just how much to tell them, what would happen if she told them the whole truth, how they would look at her and take it all, and whether they would love her the same. She had always been considered the toughest of them all. But finally, she had won the battle in her mind and had, instead, chosen to face the monster head-on. She took a deep breath and explained to her siblings why she had been going to Mr. Antonio.

Attentively they had listened, with no questions or objections, as Daniella had opened up, telling them everything and hiding little to nothing. She had burst out in tears a couple of times as she had told her story, but finally, she had made it to the end, and she was grateful she had opened up. When done, her siblings had been silent for a bit as they processed what she had said, then Tora had broken the silence by ordering some tequila shots. She had saluted Daniella's boldness for acknowledging she had a problem and seeking help. Tora had asked her other siblings not to ask any further questions and instead trust that their sister would be all right. They had all assured Daniella that they were there for her if she needed anything, and they called it a night.

That night Daniella had had a peaceful night and slept better than she had in years. The tears had eased a burden in her heart, and she had felt better for it. She had broken down one of her defense fences and told the truth, and her sibling's reactions had melted and warmed her heart. She had been surprised that she had felt more secure and protected after letting down her guard and letting her siblings in her secret. As she had woken up the following day, she had been excited to attend her next session.

The Punch and the Running

While conversing with Mr. Antonio and building rapport before the session started, Daniella told him how she had decided to sign up for kickboxing classes, which had fascinated her since she was young. Mr. Antonio was happy to see his client's progress. However, he couldn't help but wonder why he hadn't thought of going down this route and applying this method earlier or even two years ago. Daniella hadn't only looked, but she had felt much brighter than she had in a long while and had become more and more open to the idea of the guest list as the days passed. The excitement of learning more about her dream had led her to ask Mr. Antonio if his schedule had permitted her to take up more frequent sessions than their current arrangement of a maximum of two sessions a week. However, Mr. Antonio had cautioned her that while that might have been possible, he would not have recommended her to take that path as an overdose of information may not have been healthy for her.

He had further told her that just as it takes time to get a physically fit body through exercises and proper dieting, the same had applied to her mindset shift. She needed to be patient and trust the process as a habit gets built with consistent actions for it to stick. She needed to feel each moment at its own pace to move past the set beliefs in her mind. She needed not to be hasty for the results but rather practice patience. He was determined to let her embrace her past and accept it with no judgment or criticism but rather than learn from it. He had wanted her to understand where she was coming from and through that work in the present moment, which she had control over through the choices she would be making. He had further explained to her that the future may have been uncertain and could only get shaped through the actions of the present. In this session, Daniella expressed interest in learning more about what the punch in her nightmare meant or related to as they had done with the monster.

Picking up his notepad, Mr. Antonio began his line of questioning to help his client understand that part of her nightmare, "Daniella, would you mind sharing with me how it felt when you threw a punch but no results?" he had asked.

"You have no idea," she had said, closing her right hand into a fist as if ready to throw a punch. "It felt horrible!" she had continued in an elevated voice, looking down at her now-formed fist and using her left hand to cover it.

Noticing her shift in mood, Mr. Antonio decided to change his line of questioning and instead asked her if there had been anything else she needed to share about that part of her dream. This way, he had given her the space to open up and speak about anything that she felt was relevant, allowing her to feel in charge and elevate her moods.

"Uhm! Uhm! Honestly, I could not hear my thoughts. All I could hear was my heart throbbing fast as if it was an electric train on the tracks. I felt as if I was weak and powerless at that time." So, she had said, still gazing down. Gently, Mr. Antonio probed her to check if there was anything else she wanted to share. In response, Daniella softly said "no," released her fist, and stopped looking down.

Mr. Antonio had asked Daniella to take a five-minute break to get some fresh air before continuing their session. Once she had settled back from the break, he had explained to her that the lack of willpower when throwing a punch could have been because her subconscious mind had picked up her familiar pattern when tackling her issues where she had learned to compromise on things, and that had left her unfulfilled. "Talk about life being unfair!" Daniella had exclaimed. "I assume I am the only one who was dreaming of a monster chasing her. Is that even normal for a child or teenager?" She had asked with her eyebrows pulled up and together.

Mr. Antonio had smiled as if reassuring Daniella there was nothing wrong with her. Then, with a comforting voice, he had said, "You see, Daniella, for nature to balance, we cannot all be the same. I cannot explain the science behind it, but I can tell you that I hold the opinion that it is the law of nature. I am a Christian, and from the biblical point of view, in the book of Jeremiah 29:11, it does state that God does have a plan for each one of us."

Mr. Antonio had further told Daniella that just like her, millions of people were undergoing the same situation where they got fed with beliefs by the people around them or through observations in their environments. And as they grew older, they got accustomed to the thoughts. To explain further, he had said,

"You see, Daniella, our minds are like computers, and how we program them is the output they will give. Consider the thoughts as the software to your mind, which is the computer. The beauty of it is that it is possible to change our thinking patterns just like we update the software of a computer or a phone. How one looks at a situation depends on the software programs they use and, importantly, if they constantly get upgraded to the latest versions." he had said vehemently.

In response, Daniella had said, "I did not know you read the Bible. You are a man of many faces and talents."

Mr. Antonio laughed with humor before he had continued, "I take each opportunity I get to increase my knowledge seriously. Just like a car needs service now and then, my mind must also get serviced through continuous knowledge. Needless to say, knowledge is power. Anyway, back to your question, I am not sure if you have read or heard the butterfly's story. A man spent hours watching a butterfly struggling to emerge from its cocoon. It made a small hole, but its body was too large to get through. After a long struggle, it appeared exhausted and remained still. The man decided to help the butterfly. With a pair of scissors, he cut open the cocoon, thus releasing the butterfly. However, the butterfly's body was tiny and wrinkled, and its wings crumpled. The man continued to watch, hoping that, at any moment, the butterfly would open its wings and fly away. Nothing happened; the butterfly spent the rest of its brief life dragging around its lean body and shriveled wings, incapable of flight. What the man, out of kindness and in his eagerness to help, had failed to understand was that the tight cocoon and the efforts that the butterfly had to make to squeeze out of that tiny hole was nature's way of training and preparing the butterfly for life and of strengthening its wings." he had said.

"I feel bad for that butterfly but pardon my bluntness; what does that story have to do with me?" Daniella had asked.

"Good question," Mr. Antonio said with a smile as if he had wanted Daniella to ask that question. "Sometimes, a little extra effort is precisely what prepares us for the next obstacle. Anyone who refuses to make that effort, or gets the wrong sort of help, is left unprepared to fight the next battle and never manages to fly off to their destiny. You are the butterfly in this story Daniella. While it may sound ridiculous, I believe the fear of rejection you hold prepared and strengthened you for your next phase in life. Three years ago, you tried to find the right type of help by signing up for sessions with me. I know my services are not cheap," he had paused as they both chuckled, "but our progress is preparing you for the next battle as you fly off to your destiny." he had said.

Coincidentally, Daniella's favorite insect was a butterfly, and hearing she was the butterfly in the story made her glad. At that moment, she recalled how she had gone on a picnic with Jacob three years prior. She had been fascinated with the beauty and freedom of the butterflies flying around. During that time, she had opened up to him. She expressed to him just how restless and empty she had felt, despite having a flourishing career and a great relationship with him. It was then that Jacob recommended that she seek the services of a professional. He joked that that may have been what she needed to be as free as the butterflies dancing around them. He had further told her that his career coach, whom Daniella had known about since they had started dating, had been a great asset to his business's progress and success.

Daniella had reached out for her glass of beetroot juice as she had told Mr. Antonio that the idea that she had been preparing for the future had made her feel excited. Mr. Antonio then decided to give her another story of a concept referred to as elephant thinking.

"Elephant thinking is not a philosophical term, but it was a term developed from practical methods used by circus trainers to prepare their elephants," he had said in an animated tone. "The idea stems from when a baby elephant's leg gets chained to a pole on the ground," he had said while placing his pen vertically on the table and supporting it with his right hand as if to paint the picture for Daniella. At this point, Daniella had stopped crossing her legs, placed her beetroot juice down, and moved forward on the couch near the table where Mr. Antonio had the pen. "The calf tries to escape, but its efforts bear no fruit as the chain is too long and the pole is too deep in the ground." He had said and paused and used his left hand to point to the pen and an imaginary chain on the table.

Understanding what he had meant, Daniella nodded and chirped, "I bet it manages to escape when it becomes an adult."

"How I wish," Mr. Antonio had continued. With time it gives up and stops trying, wrongly assuming it cannot get away from the pole because they are stronger than it is. The elephant grows into an adult; let's say it's about six-ton. At this point, the elephant is not mighty but stronger and has enough power to escape. However, it does not try to because it has been programmed from an early age to think that escape is impossible and to believe that the rope and pole holding it in place is unshakable. Some circus trainers have pointed out that occasionally they put a piece of string around the six-ton elephant. It will not break away due to the mentality in its head, " he said, putting his pen back on his notepad.

Seemingly disappointed with the story's ending, Daniella had adjusted herself on the couch and leaned back.

"Interesting, right?" Mr. Antonio had asked.

"Not the ending I had expected, but it is quite an interesting story. Am I the elephant in this story like in the butterfly story?" she had asked humorlessly.

Noticing her eagerness, Mr. Antonio explained the lessons learned in that story and why they were important in their session.

"This assumed constraint on the elephant's ankle represents the beliefs we hold onto based on our past experiences. The beliefs we learn at an early age have somehow become determining factors as we grow up on what we can and cannot do. These beliefs have the potential to become the invisible walls in our heads that may, at times, limit us from exploring our full capabilities. They may be the inhibitors of our abilities. Of course, one may upgrade their software by going to school and reading educational materials, attending webinars and workshops, and paying for coaching sessions. Still, the problem lies in not letting go of the old software just like the adult elephant." he had said, taking a brief pause to see whether Daniella had any questions or comments.

Her silence had encouraged him to continue, "Self-inhibiting words such as 'I can't do it/this, et cetera., I am not good enough., I may get judged., I am not ready., I am worried that I will fail., this is how it should get done., someone like me cannot do this., they are better than me., if only., why me?, and many other negative statements have hindered many of us from trying things out. Despite seeking help, others have returned to the rope tied around their ankles. It is like having the intention of upgrading your software. Still, you keep using the same old software instructions repeatedly. That is why self-awareness is essential if one wants to live a different life. With self-awareness, one can focus on their emotions, actions, or thoughts and better understand why they feel in a particular way." Mr. Antonio had said.

Realizing that she had found the answer to her question, Daniella said, "I like the story of the elephant, and sitting here listening to you makes me realize I may be the six-ton elephant in my life. I have, if not all, 90% of the resources that I need, but one way or another, I always end up having the same thoughts, and, in my case, it is the doubting sentences that start with 'What if.' The worst part of it all has always been that after that conversation in my head on how I can do something, I have always ended up doing the same thing, either postponing or never doing that thing I have thought of at all. Is there a remedy for this, or how could I become better and break off the rope on my ankle?" she asked.

"I hear you, and first, I would love to reiterate that you are not alone, Daniella. As I mentioned earlier, the best remedy is self-awareness. Self-awareness entails that one focuses on themselves and understands their behavior patterns. I look at self-awareness in two ways. The first way is self-awareness which focuses on understanding the internal systems. With this, I mean being conscious and aware of how you feel towards or in certain situations, how you think, and, importantly, how you view yourself internally. You can achieve this by understanding your strengths, weaknesses, passions, priorities, et cetera. Further, understanding your internal system allows you to be aware of your impact on those around you. The second way is self-awareness of how other people view us. External awareness makes great leaders as they can practice empathy. When you get the time, check out the Johari window, designed to help increase internal and external self-awareness. With self-awareness, you can identify and work on areas that need changes. For instance, you have mentioned that you have noticed a pattern where you come up with great ideas and end up postponing or dismissing the idea. With that awareness, you need to identify what beliefs you have programmed your mind to understand, then change that to something different, something positive and self-empowering." he had explained.

Daniella seemed to be intrigued with the words from Mr. Antonio, and she had asked, "Now that makes much sense. How does one become more self-aware?"

In response, Mr. Antonio stated, "There are many ways one could do this. However, my top two suggestions could be first, meditation, a mind and body practice that focuses on the interactions between mind, body, behavior, and brain. This connection has four key elements, which include a comfortable posture, a quiet place away from distractions, an open attitude and a focus of attention. Secondly, you can make use of the Johari window that I had earlier mentioned. The Johari window is a framework designed to help one map their internal self-awareness or how well they know themselves against how well they understand how others see them or what we can call their external self-awareness." he had responded.

After that session, Mr. Antonio asked Daniella to take some time to reflect on their previous sessions. He had further asked her to write a letter to herself, expressing her feelings and addressing her fear of rejection as a person. He further explained that personifying her fears would help her see things more vividly and would help evoke her emotions while she wrote the letters. Daniella found this request weird and wondered how she could address her fear as a person. However, since the sessions had been going well and successfully, she had decided to try it and get the best value for her investment of time and money. Mr. Antonio had further asked her to take a thirty-day break as she focused on doing the reflection, after which they would resume their sessions. As a professional and from his work experience, Mr. Antonio knew that if he did not provide the breaks and let Daniella work it for herself, she would have become addicted to the sessions and might not have performed well out there on her own.

Daniella had been a bit disappointed as she was on fire and had wanted more wisdom from him. However, as Mr. Antonio had walked her out of the door to bid her goodbye, he had reminded her of his earlier warnings when she had wanted to take up more sessions that too much of something could be poisonous. Instead, he had wanted her to feel and live each moment. Daniella had then bid Mr. Antonio and his secretary goodbye, and she had gone to meet Rosa for lunch.

The Thirty Days Break

Things had been going well, and Daniella felt like a different person. Her outlook on life was changing, and she was in high spirits. Her focus was back, and she had decided to return to work. Her change had not just been internal but was visibly noticeable and acknowledged by others. Jacob, who had been supportive of her from day one and had encouraged her to seek help, had noticed too and shared in her joy. He had stuck to their original agreement and not tried to interfere with her sessions or ask her any questions about them or how they were going. He had been content to listen to her and be her sounding board when she needed as well as her shoulder to cry on when the sessions had taken a toll on her emotionally.

Jacob was not only proud of her but loved, believed, and trusted in his woman. He was her biggest cheerleader and seemed to see something in her that Daniella, for the life of her at that time, could not see. He had always made her feel secure, seen, and included. Whenever he had or would find himself at a crossroads, he would seek her opinion. His friends had taken to teasing him and would call him obsessed with Daniella as she was constantly on his lips. He would bring her up whatever conversation he was having with them. There had been a running joke amongst their peers that whenever he was down, one only had to bring up Daniella's name, and he would feel better.

Yeli had suggested a weekend getaway when the five siblings had met up for a movie night at Zee's condo. The idea seemed sane and got approved by all five of them, and they, with Jacob, Rosa, and Zee's boyfriend, had set off to Mauritius. Yeli, who had visited the small country of Mauritius more than ten times, had promised them that it was a beautiful place with endless beaches and insanely beautiful sunsets. She had confessed to them that each time she had visited, she had wanted to stay longer. So, they had a fun-filled weekend with a lot of dancing, swimming, and beach games. To Daniella's delightful surprise, there had also been a meditation instructor. Remembering Mr. Antonio's suggestion of becoming self-aware through meditation, she took advantage of the opportunity and found that she loved the feeling.

At sunset on their second day, Daniella had excused herself from the group, and Jacob, being a concerned fiancée, had followed her. She had turned him back, reassuring him she was okay and that she needed to be alone to focus and complete an assignment from Mr. Antonio. She had found a quiet place in their hotel room and, grabbing paper and sitting down at the balcony area, had begun to write in a reflective mood. She started by addressing rejection in the form of a letter as directed by Mr. Antonio, as he felt it would help her release her negative emotions and frustrations. The letter was as follows:

Dear rejection, I need to break up with you!

You are already telling me this letter is a bit cheesy, and I should stop being so sensitive. But I am going to write it anyway because I hate you. Yes, I know the look on your face when I say that, but the truth of the matter is, over the years, I have seen you for who you are and what you have done to me. You have constantly argued that you were trying to keep me safe but come on! Your methods are pretty weird, and all the voices you have ever put in my head were a lie.

Today, I am writing to inform you that I have got it from here. I am ready to try something different. I am prepared to stand head high, embrace my flaws and accept myself for who I am. Over the years, you have taught me self-doubt, and your favorite line to me has been that I am not enough. You have constantly wiped the smile off my face by being that dark cloud on a sunny day in my mind.

Yes, I am leaving you, and I want nothing more to do with you. Living with you is exhausting and impossible, for lack of a better word. You have made me sensitive, emotional, and worse off, needy with low self-esteem. You have mastered where it hurts most and double-reinforced it, but today, I have some news for you. I have finally realized the damage you have done to me by depriving me of living and embracing the best version of myself, and I loathe you for that. You are a terrible habit in my head, and I want you to pack and leave. I no longer need your shady services. It is time for a new chapter in my life, and there is no room or space for you.

I have not given up on myself, and it is time for me to let the caterpillar in me blossom into a butterfly. I will love myself more, venture into my dreams, have better relationships, and be happy. Please respect my wishes, as I want you out of my life.

Regards, Daniella

Daniella had folded the letter and put it inside her handbag before returning and rejoining the group. She had ordered some tequila shots, and the party had begun. It had been as if she had been reborn that evening. She had felt different, light as a feather, and she was no longer as burdened. She had danced under the moon to her heart's content, and a big smile crossed her face. Over the years, when the siblings were together, Tora had always been the life of the party, but on this night, Daniela had surprised them as she had taken the role. "Was she supposed to celebrate after asking for a break-up?" She had wondered to herself.

Jacob had been watching her while seated at the bar counter and enjoying a cold beer. He had been amazed at how she danced freely under the moon dressed in Sari, a Mauritius traditional dress that brought out her body curves beautifully. After he had proposed to her, they had agreed to wait to set the date until Daniella had found the peace and clarity she had been searching for. He had wanted to give her space and not pressure her. However, that evening watching her, he had felt that he could not wait any longer to have her as his wife, so he had taken Daniella on the side and expressed himself and what he had felt. Daniella had agreed with him, and they had set the date and announced it to the group. That news had cheered everyone more and had given them more reasons to celebrate. That night had marked a significant moment in Daniella's life. She had woken up the following day to the worst hangover. Still, even that fact could not take away from the feeling of being free in her, as she had not only faced her greatest fear of rejection but she had also so much to look forward to and much to be grateful for.

During the thirty-day break, Daniella had taken the initiative to write out even more letters to deal with her fears. In one of such letters, she had addressed it to pleaser, where she had dealt with her urge to please everyone at the expense of her peace of mind. While writing this letter, she had thought back to two relationships that had turned toxic but dragged on out of fear.

Dear pleaser,

First, I know not to be deceived by your name anymore. Second, I know that just like rejection, you, too, are upset that the day has finally come when I have become aware of your existence and what you do in my life. You seduced me into believing I needed society's approval to live a fulfilled life.

From a young age, you made me think that the opinions of others mattered. You made me forget myself as I worked hard to please everyone else. Anytime confidence tried to knock on the door; you always made sure to answer the door and lie that it had the wrong address. I remember when I was 18 years old, I was trying so hard to please a group of teenagers in my neighborhood. Being the recruit, I got asked to do something I was not proud of. Deep down, I knew I had the choice to say no, but the desire to fit in and not be the loner kicked in. I really wanted to trust my gut feeling and stay away from them.

Around the age of 22, confidence had managed to slip your tight security and convinced me that it did not matter, as I never needed everyone's approval. Confidence made a case, and deep down, I knew the points presented made sense. Then, two days later, you showed up, filled my head with nonsense things, and took me back under your spell.

Please pack up and leave my life for good. I want to be free of your spell. I don't want or need you anymore.

Regards, Daniella

One morning, Daniella received an email from a potential client. Once she had read it, she knew she would have made money if the client had approved her proposed deal. She had been excited and started drafting the email with the proposal. However, she began to doubt herself between drafting her proposal and hitting the send button. Her mind had become swamped with "what if" thoughts. Getting increasingly overwhelmed, Daniella closed her laptop and moved from her workstation. She decided to fill the time by meditating, a new habit she had employed and would do in her office. During those thirty minutes of meditation, she became aware of self-doubt and wrote a letter addressing it.

Dear self-doubt

From a young age, you made sure your children and grandchildren fed properly from me. Anytime a great idea started growing in me; you would blow that candle out, making me hesitant to take most actions. I have watched my friends grow with the idea that came from me, and since I did not act fast enough, they beat me to it. You have made me feel worthless and not good enough. The more I wanted to resist your charms, the more you kept growing in me. How could you? You robbed me of my self-esteem over and over.

Despite establishing my name in the industry as an adult, you have often snuck in and nourished the seeds you planted years ago. Now that I think of it, I know you like grand entrances and the red carpet, as whenever you pop up, I always have a significant project at hand. An excellent example is last year when I launched the free photography academy for the youths. You made me doubt myself, doubt whether I was capable of doing a great job or not. Last year because of listening to you, I almost canceled the launch, something that has turned out to be a blessing to the youths. Honestly, I cannot even count the times I have procrastinated and delayed things because of you.

I can list down a thousand things you have done in my life that are not impressive. I want you and your entire generation to pack and leave me alone. I am in charge of my life, and I know I can do great things without pressure from others, including you. So kindly leave and never come back. I have laid down the red carpet for your grand exit. I am done!

Regards, Daniella

Daniella had felt good after writing that letter. She had felt empowered, and returning to her email, she had hit the send button. Two days later, she received a response for the initial meet-up to finalize the details. As the days progressed, Daniella found it easier to face her other bad habits. So, she wrote out the following letters to hatred and insecurities.

Dear hatred,

First of all, you are pretty treacherous. I have been taught in Sunday school to forgive and forget, but how come I hold ill feelings toward some people? How come I cannot stand to be in the presence of some people? I forgave them for what they did to me, but why are you forcing me to despise them?

You have done a proper job nourishing the seeds you planted. You clearly know that from a young age, all I wanted was to fit in, but you are working hard to sabotage my efforts. Some grudges

I hold have no basis. Even worse are the behaviors that have developed in me as a defense mechanism, such as aggression. I am polite and do not like what you are doing to me.

Over the years, you have shadowed yourself behind self-doubt and rejection, and it's not until now that I have realized that you exist in my life. Are you the reason my heart feels heavy with an unexplainable burden? You know what, don't answer me. All I want is for you to pack and leave me alone. In your place, I will welcome love who will teach me what it really means to forgive and forget. With professional help, I will also learn and master the skill of dissociation. Kindly exit my life.

Regards, Daniella.

Dear insecurities

I have always been a brilliant girl. However, you have provided an imbalance in my life from a young age. You are making me focus on what I am not getting rather than what I have. You are nerve-wracking and painful, and over the years, you have made me believe that I am not worthy of love and care.

Do you remember Timmy? For the longest time, I always blamed him for leaving me for another woman. How could he not? I was that nagging girlfriend who always wanted to know his whereabouts every minute. Each time we were not together, all I could think of was that he was cheating on me. Jealousy had become my second name; half the time, we were always in a fight triggered by you. Finally, I pushed him out of my life, and I blame you for that. Timmy was a good man, and you cost me years of happiness.

You have manifested yourself in my relationships and have cost me great connections that would have led to good business.

I want you to detach from my life completely. I want you to pack and leave. Kindly shut the door behind you. Just like Timmy replaced me with the new princess in our love fairy tale, I replace you with self-confidence. Yes, payback is here. Get out!

Regards, Daniella

After the 30 Days Break

"Are you pregnant, Daniella?" Mr. Antonio had jokingly asked when Daniela had walked into his office for their session.

She had been caught off-guard by the question, but when she had looked at his face and noticed he was merely teasing her, she had jokingly responded with an "Is it that obvious?" back to him.

After Daniella had settled on the couch, Mr. Antonio had gone to find out how her thirty-day break had been. In response, Daniella had explained to him how she had gone and written more letters after addressing rejection as he had previously asked her. She had further pulled out an envelope from her handbag and told him with a smile that she had placed all the letters in that envelope. Mr. Antonio had then explained to Daniella that writing down the letters had been the tip of the iceberg. She needed to take actions that would enable her to fully detach from all those behavior patterns she had addressed in her letters. He'd explained to her that writing the letters was like removing weeds from a garden; if one did not make it a constant habit, the weeds would grow back up and ruin the garden. He had further asked Daniella to carry the envelope and accompany him to the fireplace in his office. He had then asked her to burn the letters to help release the emotional ties with those traits.

After the exercise, they settled back into their respective seating places. Together, they devised a daily routine that Daniella would follow. In this routine, she would always think of the outcome and ask herself three specific questions:

1. What worst scenario could happen when I take this action?
2. What is the best scenario that could happen when I take this action?
3. What is my choice?

Mr. Antonio explained to Daniella that an outcome is like setting a goal. Once one has a plan, one can program their activities toward achieving it. Having the outcome in mind helped shape one's behavior. One could decide whether their actions justified the outcome by asking the three questions. Furthermore, he had told Daniella that by being aware of her outcomes, she would guard them by taking the necessary actions regardless of whatever emotions crept in to stop her. He'd advised her to start with small daily steps that would form the foundation of her journey, such as having a tracker that she would update daily on the progress.

In addition, Mr. Antonio had asked Daniella if she believed in the words she had written down in her letters. In response, Daniella had said, "I believe in the words I have written down in those letters. However, sometimes during the thirty-day break, I felt like I was doubting Thomas when I saw the envelope."

Mr. Antonio had thanked her for her honesty before he had asked her, "May I ask what your description or understanding is of a doubting Thomas?"

Daniella seemed preoccupied with her thoughts before answering, "I describe him as the person behind me, not taking action whenever required to. Sometimes I have great plans in my head, but before I put them down, he has already come in and made me rethink and wonder if that idea was as great as I thought it was."

Mr. Antonio had written down something on his notepad before he said, "That is quite interesting, Daniella. Have you read the story of the doubting Thomas in the Bible and the conditions that led him to get branded that name?"

Without hesitation, Daniella answered, "Yes, I do remember when I was young, we read that story in church."

Happy that they were on the same page, Mr. Antonio said, "There are two sides to a coin, so let us assume the same applies to doubting Thomas. From my research, there are many historians, scientists, and theologians alike who actually consider that Thomas was being logical, cautious, and wise in demanding evidence. He would not be comfortable just taking in what everyone said without being sure of himself. With this line of thinking, what comes to mind when you returned to those occasions when you did not act because you doubted yourself?" He had asked.

Daniella had deliberated over what Mr. Antonio had said before she had answered, "Well, if I think of things that way, then I would say that those occasions when I felt I was doubting Thomas were moments I was reminding myself to conduct research and not what I have been doing over the years," she had paused tucking her braided hair behind her right ear before she had concluded with a silent sigh and said, "stopping and not doing the due diligence before dismissing an idea."

Noticing that Daniella had drifted away in thoughts, Mr. Antonio had remained silent for about 5 minutes before he said, "Brilliant explanation Daniella; shift of mindset is significant in our everyday lives. When faced with situations, we have two choices. One choice is to run and give in, and the other is to ask simple, thought-provoking questions to help us dissect the situation. Questions such as 'What is the meaning of this thought?' helps one to create a pros and cons list, which in turn gives a better understanding of the thought. A mindset shift is dominantly how we think. It gets achieved by challenging our limiting beliefs, changing negative self-talk, and shifting perspective as we have done with doubting Thomas. One could also get support from a professional coach or mentor who has walked the path."

Before their session ended, Mr. Antonio explained his next assignment to Daniella. She would form a committee that had a minimum of 8 and a maximum of 10 members. He had then explained to her that the committee would consist of the values she had wanted to be associated with and personify them just like she had done with her fears. The activity would help her evoke her emotions. She would then clearly state why she needed each value and welcome them into her life. He had given her an example of how she would structure her invitation letters using love, and he said, "Hey love, I desire to be associated with you. I want to understand your true intentions in my life. I welcome you into my life. Please accept my invitation to be part of the committee." Mr. Antonio's example had drawn a blank stare from Daniella, and he had then decided to expound more on that topic.

"I love works and books by others to garner more wisdom and expand my own. I learned this method when I read a book from Napoleon Hill, 'Think and Grow Rich.' In one of the book's chapters, Napoleon explained how one could build character through autosuggestion." he had paused, stood up from the two-seater couch where he had been sitting and had walked past Daniella to his bookshelf behind the three-seater couch. He had then picked up the book by Napoleon and had sat down before reading to Daniella the definition of autosuggestion from the book:

"Autosuggestion is the agency of control through which an individual may voluntarily feed his subconscious mind on thoughts of creative nature, or, by neglect, permit thoughts of a destructive nature to find their way into this rich garden of the mind." Napoleon Hill.

Daniella had nodded in understanding, and Mr. Antonio had continued, "According to Napoleon, one can build their character through their dominating thoughts and desires, and with every deeply rooted desire has the consequence of making one seek outward expression through which that desire may get converted into reality, and this could get achieved through self-suggestion. Thus, with this knowledge, Napoleon had formed imaginary council meetings where he would call his cabinet members for the knowledge, he had wished each would contribute and would address himself to each member in audible words." Mr. Antonio had paused, taking a sip from his glass of water while giving room to Daniella if she had any questions or comments. Daniella had been nodding and seemed curious to hear more about this committee forming.

Mr. Antonio continued, "From my understanding of the book, with building character, one can use both human and nonhuman cabinet members. In my case, when I was a young man back in my university days and was trying to find my purpose in life, I formed my first committee, which consisted of great coaches such as Robin Sharma and Jay Shetty, among others. I also invited personality figures such as Nelson Mandela. I selected them because I admired their personalities and how they led their lives. I would then find a private time when my roommate was away for classes and enjoy the secluded time by addressing myself to each cabinet member in audible words. I sometimes asked their opinions and what they would do in certain situations. As this is all imaginary, I had to pay attention by closing my eyes to avoid distractions.

The majority of the qualities I sought from my committee came to reality. I asked Jay Shetty and Robin to pass their knowledge so that I can help people globally, and well, here we are today, Daniella. Through Nelson Mandela, I overcame the desire to fight whenever someone offended me or did not do as I expected. Through the cabinet's imaginary conversations, I learned that violence was not the answer and that forgiving overpowers self-pity, among other things. I had also made it my mission to study their life histories and personalities as that would help me when having imaginary meetings." He had said.

Mr. Antonio's explanation seemed to have fascinated Daniella. In response, she had said, "Wow! That is a lot to take in and a lot of lessons for one to learn. How did it feel when you had your first cabinet meeting?" she had asked.

In response, Mr. Antonio had said, "At first, it did not sit well with me as it was a new venture, but with time, it started becoming natural as I had promised myself to at least hold the imaginary meetings at least once a week. As you know, with practice, things get better.

"As he spoke, Daniella was staring at the book that Mr. Antonio had been holding, and she had said, "I should rekindle my love for reading works of others. Maybe I should get book referrals from you, too." she had said, looking at Mr. Antonio with expectant eyes.

"You see that wall behind you?" Mr. Antonio had said, pointing to the bookshelf behind Daniella, and she had turned her whole body to follow his gesture, "It holds almost a thousand books that I have read. Each book with special notes from my understanding of the book. And amazingly, I get new insights every time I re-read a book. I am one person who believes that learning is a weapon everyone can use to build themselves up. One can start with the publications within reach. Once you make reading fun, you find yourself reading even more. Your brain will and does feed on the food you give it. However, I should caution you to be careful of what you allow your brain to consume. Strive to feed your brain with positive thoughts, ideas, and things, as this is a seed that you are planting. I am happy to lend them to you. You can make this your mini library." he chuckled.

At this time, Daniella had stood up and walked to the bookshelf and started touching the books as if she was looking for one in particular before she said, "Thank you, Mr. Antonio. I am glad I knocked on your door 3 years ago." she had spoken with a smile before she walked back to the couch and sat down.

After that session, Mr. Antonio gave her the book Think and Grow Rich so she could understand more about forming the committee. After that, he asked her to take another break from the sessions to create a proper committee and, once ready, schedule an appointment with him. After bidding him goodbye, Daniella drove to the supermarket and bought her favorite wine and some cooking ingredients. She had then gone home and prepared herself a long hot bath that lasted almost thirty minutes. She then made a delicious meal for herself that consisted of Ugali (Cornmeal), Sukuma Wiki (kale), Nyama Choma (grilled meat), and some Kachumbari (an uncooked salad dish consisting of fresh tomatoes, cucumbers, and onions). After having her dinner, she had then decided to start reading the book. Before she had known it, she was dead asleep, being a Friday; she had been weary from the week's work.

The Wedding Planning

Having set the date, Daniella had been under immense pressure to organize the wedding. It was to be her one big shot, her one special day, and she had wanted it to be perfect. While this had been her intention, Daniella had found that she had been getting carried away with her sessions with Mr. Antonio and had, unfortunately, often showed up late for any wedding plan appointments. Despite being as understanding and patient as Jacob could be, he found that his patience started to run thin when Daniella completely forgot and missed their cake-tasting appointment. However, he still understood how vital the sessions were to her, so he suggested they postpone the wedding and move it to a different date so she would not spread herself too thin. Daniella noted the disappointment in his voice, and she had been reluctant to postpone the wedding. She had been quick to reject the idea and had instead promised Jacob that she would better manage her time.

To avoid being carried away and missing other important appointments, Daniella bought herself a daily planner that she had intended would assist her in becoming more organized. She had also decided to employ a personal assistant to remind her of the major appointments and sort her daily activities. Aside from work and wedding planning-related appointments, Daniella had also decided that she would free up some time for her to do other activities, such as going for a walk or running to catch up with nature and jet skiing.

Daniella had wanted an elegant wedding, and her committee, which had consisted of her sisters and best friend Rosa, had promised to make her dream come true. As part of the planning, they distributed the roles among themselves. Zee had been in charge of overseeing the wedding gown and all other fashion-related stuff. Tora had offered the club backyard for the reception and after party as it had a great view overlooking the mountains and the town's lake. Yeli, the wanderer, had been appointed to arrange their traveling plans, while Rosa had been in charge of printing the wedding advertisements and the program. As a group, they had all been responsible for ensuring Daniella did not get carried away with other things and forget to plan for her wedding. It had been an exciting adventure for the five of them as they had found an excuse to leave town and travel worldwide, sourcing things for the wedding. In one of their escapades, they had ended up in Vegas, the city of lights, and they had decided to have a teaser bachelorette party. There had been only one rule for that night; whatever had happened in Vegas had to remain in Vegas. Between the five of them, the events of that night had to be kept secret and not spoken to any soul ever.

The Selection of Values

It had been a month of moving back and forth since Daniella's last session with Mr. Antonio. Finally, she had managed to read the book that he had lent her, and she better understood what he had meant by identifying values that would form her imaginary committee. Throughout the month, she had tried to come up with her unique values; however, her efforts had been fruitless. It was not until the fifth Sunday since her last session with Mr. Antonio that she had woken up feeling energetic and psyched up to select members of her to be imaginary committee. The previous evening, she had spent at a friend's birthday party, where there had been a lot of fun games that included Truth or Dare and Spin the Bottle, among others.

Daniella had found an idea from the party's games and had decided to use that idea to select her values. She had written down all the qualities she thought she needed for her imaginary committee and had a total of twenty-five. As had been instructed by Mr. Antonio, Daniella had to narrow down to at least ten from the twenty-five, and she had decided to borrow an idea from spin the bottle game. She had decided to write down the twenty-five values on a sticky note paper and had circularly arranged them on the floor. She had then decided in her version of the game that she would alter the conventional rules of the game and instead place a bottle in the center of her newly formed circle with the sticky note papers and spin it. The sticky note paper that the sealing surface of the bottle pointed to would become one of her final select values. She had found an old perfume bottle in her closet and had begun the game. Once set and everything had been in place, Daniella had put on loud techno music, spun the bottle, and danced every time the bottle stopped. If you had been watching her, you would have thought she had lost it. Within ten minutes, she had her winners and had taken her laptop, and had written her invitation letters to her imaginary committee as follows:

Hey, confidence; I desire to build my character and put my trust in you more. As you may have heard, I tend to shy away from things out of fear of rejection or what other people might say or think about me. I constrict myself from aiming higher or making hard, bold moves because you are somehow missing in my life. I know you have made countless efforts to try and come into my life, but rejection has been kicking you out. Good news, I have kicked rejection out of my life, and I want to have 100% trust in you. So, I welcome you to be part of my committee for you to always stand by my side and remind me always to trust myself. I hope you will accept my invitation.

Hey, happiness, I request to acquire from your positive emotions in both my mental and emotional states. I desire the freedom of having joy and contentment in my daily activities. I want to laugh and feel fulfilled. Honestly, the last time I went for a comedy night, I thought there was something wrong with me because while everyone else was laughing hard to the point of shedding tears, I could not see the humor in any of it. I was bored, and now that I think of it, I need you to ignite that spark in me. Over the years, as I have guarded my heart, I also locked you out. I invite you to be part of my committee, stick by my side and give me that glow that I see in other people. Please accept my invitation.

Hey, self-control, I implore you to join my committee as the chairman. I desire to make rational decisions from the bottom of my heart. I can only achieve this by having you by my side to remind me that I control my emotions, thoughts, and temptations. I have heard how you have helped millions of people achieve specific goals, and I desire to have that in my life too. I know you have seen my pattern, where I say Yes when I clearly wanted to say No, which has cost my business thousands of dollars. It has cost me my dignity, and as I write this letter of invitation to you, I am struggling to express my feelings and emotions toward other people. I really want you by my side, and I hope you will accept my invitation.

Hey, forgiveness; having learned in Sunday school that the Bible says we should forgive seventy times seven times a day, I thought I had acquired this skill automatically. I desire to learn from you what it means to forgive someone genuinely. Whenever I judge someone based on what they have done to me, I want you to step in and fill my heart with compassion, empathy, and understanding. I want to let go of the feelings of resentment and vengeance that I hold in my heart. I also want to learn the art of self-forgiveness and letting go of the past. I know you want to help me, and I cannot wait for you to join the committee.

Hey, self-awareness, sometimes, I am fully aware of who I am, but I get lost in my bubble on other occasions. I desire to have you on my side. I want you to train me to be focused on myself, understand my actions, thoughts, and emotions, and whether or not they align with my standards. I want to know why I behave in a certain way sometimes. I was hoping you could give me the freedom to have clarity and change things about myself that don't align with the standards I want to be associated with. So please accept my invitation and help me transform into the butterfly I should be.

Hey, ambition; when I look back at my career progress, you have existed in my life in one way or another. You have teamed up with creativity and have done wonders since the launch of my career. However, recently, I have noticed my imagination has reduced; it is as if you are fading. I welcome you to join my committee and remind me of my goals. I was hoping you could help me build back my desire to continue being the best in the industry. I implore you not to fade away but to instead start manifesting yourself in me. I can't wait to see you at the board meetings.

Hey, honor, I invite you to join my committee. While I may have significant influence, I honestly feel I did not correctly get that. Initially, I built my business venture and became unstoppable. Part of my intention was to punish those who had made me feel inferior in the past. Unfortunately, my choices for the business were without honor. Please join my committee, so my actions transform into more honest, fair, and worthy of respect. I want to do the right thing and live up to the principles of truth. I want to be respected because I deserve it and not for other reasons. I want to have integrity. Please accept my invitation to join my committee.

Hey, honesty, I need you on my team. From a young age, I have not been telling the truth. I have been lying to those around me and myself. Part of the lies have saved me, but the other big part has drowned me. Please join my committee to remind me of the benefits of having integrity. Please remind me that it is okay to speak the truth and believe that the other person will understand me. I want you to tell me whenever I get cold feet that I can never make everyone happy. Please remind me to make myself happy and my actions honest, speaking and living by the truth. This way, I will not need to memorize and keep up with all the lies I give. It will free up more space for important things like my work and family. I urge you not to turn down my invitation.

Hey, consistency, I need your charms around me. As you know, I am in the habit of starting things, and halfway to the end, I either stop and postpone or quit. Please help me maintain my calm whenever I start a project, help me complete it, and stay focused so that I don't stop, procrastinate or quit. I can be very motivated, which has always pushed me to start a project, but I lack you. I pray you will join my committee and teach me about your great qualities.

While drafting her letter to her next imaginary committee member, Daniella remembered part of her session with Mr. Antonio a year prior, where he had shared information from an article he had read. That article explained that recent research had brought forth findings that human beings had three brains. The first brain that people pay attention to is the head, and the second and third that people may or may not be aware of are the heart and gut brain. He further explained to her the roles of the three brains as described in the article, where he stated: "When making decisions, we employ one of our three brains or all three together. We use our head, considered the rational brain that logically looks at things. We can also employ our heart the emotional brain, and look at things through passion, creativity, and feelings. Finally, the gut, also called the intuitive brain, sends unclear and implicit messages about what is going on. The little voice that whispers that something is wrong or right without telling us the reason why." Having this knowledge, Daniella had wanted to have all three work harmoniously and, thus, had invited coordination to be part of her imaginary committee. In her invitation, she had written:

Hey, coordination, I need your help understanding the balance between my head, gut, and heart brains. By doing so, I believe that I will make better decisions that will consist of creativity, emotional balance, and self-preservation. So please accept my letter of invitation to join my committee.

Daniella was on a roll, and she had felt powerful. After writing to her ten imaginary committee members, she decided to take a break and go for a walk. She had been proud of herself for finally getting that task done. Through the letters, as she spoke to her inner self, something unexplainable had happened. She had felt like a new person and was ready to book a session with Mr. Antonio for more insights. That afternoon Daniella had the cake tasting with Jacob. She had decided to surprise Jacob to make up for the earlier cake tasting she had forgotten to turn up for. She went by her local salon, where she got her hair, facial, manicure, and pedicure done. She wanted to make an effort and blow her fiancé's proverbial sock off. She chose to wear a red bodycon dress, knowing red was Jacob's favorite color on her, and opted for gold heels. She turned up at the tasting on time, to Jacobs' surprise. She could tell he was impressed with how she looked by the way he beamed at her from across the room and quickly made his way to her. Jacob could not help but announce to the room, "This is the woman I am going to marry," Daniella blushed, and the caterers laughed. After the cake tasting, Daniella spent the afternoon with Jacob. They talked about the wedding plans, where they would live as a married couple, their honeymoon, and other normal things that couples talk about in preparation for their stay together as a married couple.

Two days after the cake-tasting session, Daniella had booked her appointment with Mr. Antonio. Daniella had been excited to share her newly formed committee, but Mr. Antonio had stopped her and had told her that the committee had to be a secret that she alone was privy to. He had explained to her that the committee members, in this case, values were like the golden codes provided to the president of the United States that allowed him to authorize a nuclear attack. They were her weapon, and only she was allowed to be aware of their existence. Together, Daniella and her imaginary committee members would hold meetings at least one or two times a week and discuss major arising issues. Daniella had then expressed her concern and needed further clarification on how the sessions would have proceeded.

"It is all in your mind, Daniella, and you will need to program this process in your mind. At first, it might be difficult, funny, and weird, but with time it will get better, and it will all be worth it. A good example I can give you is by using a child. A child is scared of taking the first step. Still, with time they start walking by supporting themselves with an adult or furniture around them, and eventually, with time, they get to walk with no support at all. This success happens because, with the attempts made for walking with the support, they tend to program this in their mind and slowly build up their confidence." Mr. Antonio had explained.

Daniella then asked Mr. Antonio, "Is there a pattern on how the meetings should go?"

He had responded, "I believe you have selected the different values you want to rekindle back into your life and be associated with. You will have a specific topic to address in each meeting and ask for their insights. For instance, you could say you want to talk about a work meeting that will happen. What is the advice from your committee? Are there specific details they would like you to remember during the meeting?" Then, noticing Daniella's dazed look of bewilderment, he asked her to share one value she had listed for him to demonstrate what he had meant.

Daniella had put her left hand under her chin, supporting it with her right hand before she had said, "Well, I do have Confidence as a member," then she had placed both hands on her lap.

Mr. Antonio then stared at the bookshelf behind Daniella's couch for a minute as if pondering what Daniella had said before he said, "Thank you for sharing that name, Daniella. Going back to our example of the work meeting, you could ask for confidence insights on the matter. I assume part of the advice to you would be to go in head up, keeping in mind that they are all human beings just like you. Be prepared by understanding your presentation and being open-minded to any questions raised. Keep in mind that you may not have all the answers to questions raised, and therefore during these moments, remember not to mumble words but instead speak out clearly and inform your audience that you need more time to address that question, thus, showing them that you are in charge."

Daniella had seemed to understand Mr. Antonio's explanation of the pattern that the meetings could follow as she had said, nodding her head, "I understand." Then, with a concerned voice, she had asked, "Will I not look like a mad person when holding the imaginary committee meetings?"

Mr. Antonio had put his writing pad on the table before he had said, "Not at all, as you do this in privacy away from distractions as you need utmost concentration. As I had mentioned before, I did my imaginary meetings when my university roommate had left the room, and I was all alone. Therefore, the best time I would advise would be the evening before bed. You may not have a productive meeting in the morning as you rush to start the day; however, it depends on your schedule." Daniella had then proceeded to ask the length of the meetings, and in response, he had advised her to keep them short for better impact.

As Daniella had no further questions, they called that session to an end, and Mr. Antonio bid her goodbye.

The Gratitude Session

It had been three weeks since their last session. Daniella had told Mr. Antonio that she had become acclimated to writing letters to address all the negative habits she had wanted to kick out of her life. The progress had been good so far. Daniella had then told him that she had seen a post on Pinterest where someone had mentioned something about gratitude, and she had been interested to learn more about gratitude. Mr. Antonio then picked up his notepad and asked her, "Tell me, Daniella, what is the first thing you do when you wake up in the morning?"

Daniella had beamed a mischievous smile before she had said, "Well, it varies depending on if I woke up on time. On a good day, I check my social media to see what's trending or if I have been tagged anywhere in the blogs, after which I shower, have my breakfast, then head out and run the day's errands."

Mr. Antonio had smiled before he had said, "I hear you, Daniella. Did you know that we are faced with choices every day after we wake up?" he had asked her, and in response, Daniella had said with a contemplative look, "I believe yes as we have to choose to get out of bed or continue to sleep."

Mr. Antonio had nodded in agreement with her before he had said, "You are right, and to add on that, a great part of how our day goes depends on the first thoughts we get in our head after we rise and shine. You have the choice to get yourself in a great mood for the day and vice versa. If you woke up and let us, say you see on social media loads of accidents and death, chances are your day may be filled with a negative attitude. While if you woke up and see weddings and other happy events, your mood channels toward that energy. A good example we can use to elaborate more is what you mentioned earlier on checking whether the blogs had something to say about you. Out of curiosity, what happens when you find a negative blog about you?"

"The truth is, I tend to believe that they do not bother me, but now that I think of it, somehow I do get agitated, and when I go to the office, I am in such a bad state that my employees avoid crossing paths with me." she had said with a frown on her face.

"That's all right," Mr. Antonio had said after writing something on his notepad, "Based on your explanation, you will realize what I mean by saying you have no control over posts on social media, but you do have control over when you wish to absorb that information." he had said.

Instantaneously with a disbelief look, Daniella had asked, "In today's digital world, are you suggesting I start buying newspapers?"

In response, Mr. Antonio had laughed in humor and said, "Well, at least you will have saved your eyes and given them more life." Daniella had seemed not to understand the humor, and Mr. Antonio had continued, "What I mean is that I want to introduce to you the concept of morning gratitude recitals or what other people refer to as affirmations. Each morning after you wake up, I want you to have at least ten things you are grateful for and say them out loud so that you can hear yourself. This exercise will help remind you of how much you are blessed. Sometimes it helps provide solutions to some problems you may be facing, as expressing yourself loudly allows you to become more aware of what is going on in your mind. The morning affirmations also empower you as you become in charge as the short sentences you make influence your conscious and subconscious mind."

There was silence in the office, and Daniella seemed deep in thought before she asked, "Now that makes better sense. However, to be clear, I understood right on your explanation. Are you talking about material things only?"

In response, Mr. Antonio had said, "It could be anything, Daniella. For instance, my top 3 include being grateful for life, Grateful that my business is thriving, and grateful for all my clients. You can also mix the list with positive attitude reminders such as "I am going to have a great day." Simple words, yet they carry the weight of an elephant. You need to believe and let the words sink in as you recite these. Affirmations help build resilience; the more you recite these positive statements, the more you realize positive changes in your life."

"Ooh! Wow! That sounds interesting." Daniella had said with a smile, "Are you seriously saying that if I recite the affirmations and then later see the negative feedback, it will not affect my moods and day in general?" she asked.

Careful not to misdirect his client, Mr. Antonio said, "Yes, that is correct. You direct your intentions for the day with affirmations toward your best version. An affirmation like 'I can remain calm even when they post negative comments about me' might anchor you to a habit of deep breathing when you start to feel your blood boil. An affirmation like 'I am great at my job; I understand my skills, and I know critics help me to learn the areas I need improvement' shifts your mindset whenever you encounter that negative comment. Instead of focusing on who and why questions which automatically lead to blaming games, you start focusing on 'what can I do to improve in this area?' Always remember that your positive and negative thoughts determine many of your actions. When you believe them, they penetrate deep into your conscious and subconscious mind, building your resilient abilities and self-confidence. Importantly, Daniella, it is not just about reciting the words but also believing in them, which will make an immense difference."

Daniella had seemed thrilled with the new information, "I can think of a hundred things I am grateful for," she had said with a dampened smile with her eyes looking up to her right.

Mr. Antonio had then responded "Perfect, one step at a time. I want you to go home and write at least ten of them and recite them each morning before you get out of bed. Remember to believe the words you utter and watch your days transform." He then asked Daniella if she had questions before they finished their session. Daniella stroked her chin with her left hand and asked, "I just have one quick question, do morning affirmations help with stress management?"

"That's an excellent question," Mr. Antonio had said in response to her question, "When it comes to stress management, that's a whole topic we can look into in one of our next sessions. However, affirmations are just the tip of the iceberg regarding stress management. They do help, but there are other tools you can use together with the affirmations to build a stronger wall." He had said.

Before bidding him goodbye, Daniella had expressed her desire to learn more about stress management in their next session, and Mr. Antonio had nodded in agreement.

That evening, Daniella started writing down her top ten. When she reached number five, she realized she had forgotten the importance of family bonding. So, she stopped writing down the list and called her siblings, her fiancée, and her best friend for a slumber party at her house. She was grateful to have a supportive team who happened to be her family. The final list was as follows:

I am grateful for life and my business.

I am in charge of how I feel and choose to feel happy.

I am not a failure; I am learning from each opportunity.

I am worthy of love from others, and support surrounds me in abundance.

I am grateful for my family, my fiancée, and Rosa.

I am grateful for the vast opportunities the universe has placed for me today.

I accept myself for who I am with no judgment or criticism.

I am responsible for the thoughts that I allow in my mind.

I will not pretend to be anyone or anything other than who I am.

I am capable of making intelligent decisions for myself today.

I have all I need to make today a great day.

Over the next couple of months, Daniella strove to live by the new routine she had formed. She had become more creative in her work, and business was booming. She had also developed a system that helped her effectively balance time between family, friends, and work. Extraordinarily without knowing it, Daniella started reaching out to the people in her list of 100. For some, it was mainly for-business collaborations, while for others, it was just for casual coffee dates to catch up.

Bonus Techniques for Stress Management

Mr. Antonio observed Daniella as she walked into his office for their session. She seemed happy and radiated positive energy. He knew Daniella had experienced the changes since they started working together. She had accepted the change and embraced an open mind. But, on the other hand, he could not help but be proud of himself for a well-done job. He had always believed that his clients should get value for their money when working with him. Daniella had seated on the three-seater couch, and for about five minutes, they discussed how cold the weather was that day. Mr. Antonio's secretary had also served them coffee before she had locked the door on her way out to allow them to have their privacy. Mr. Antonio had then settled on the two-seater couch and had checked with Daniella if she had still been interested in more details on stress management or if she had something else, she wanted to discuss instead. Daniella nodded and said, "No, today I came in ready to learn stress management."

Mr. Antonio then picked up his notepad and glanced over the material he had prepared on stress management. Then he said, "You see, Daniella, I believe that stress is something that our thoughts create. In most cases, we find that it was not the situation that upset us. Rather it was our interpretation of that situation. Before I did my coaching training, my girlfriend at the time used to pick fights with me at any chance she got, or so I thought. These assumed fights would stress me and consume my productivity time, and they would drag on for days. Later on, after we split, I realized that each of us had created a mental picture of how an argument and correction should look. Whenever I did something incorrectly, like not putting my socks in the laundry basket, she would make me aware of what I had done with a high tone at that time. My thoughts would automatically pick that as an argument, so I would react with a raised voice that would offend her, and then a real argument would erupt. If I had learned how to manage and filter information that became my thoughts, I would have picked up on the fact that she was not looking for an argument but was correcting me, and this would have saved me from the time that I spent stressed over that situation and money that I spent buying apology gifts. Not to mention, she was a great woman. She probably would have been the love of my life, but after our split, she met another guy who quickly discovered her greatness and married within a year." Mr. Antonio had taken a sip from the hot coffee. Then he continued, "From my story, you can see that when we allow our emotions to control and cloud our thoughts, we lose great things. One excellent method that you can use to manage stress is by asking yourself these two questions:

Is it in my control?

Is it beyond me?

When you ask yourself these questions, you get to analyze the situation. Instead of falling into the usual stress pattern, you end up asking yourself more thought-provoking questions, such as:

What can I do? Especially if something is within your control?

What resources do I need? This question allows you to go into a resourceful state.

What can I do to make things better? Especially if things are beyond your control.

And so many other questions will make you more resourceful that I will email you for reference," he had said, seemingly enjoying his cup of coffee.

Daniella seemed to understand part of the proposed method on stress management and had been interested to understand the other part. Cautiously, she had said, "I am sorry to hear about your girlfriend, Mr. Antonio. I know how it feels to lose someone you care about, especially when you realize it is over, at times, due to lame misunderstandings. However, could you please clarify how I can make things better if something is beyond me?" she had asked.

Putting his cup of coffee down, Mr. Antonio said, "To answer your question, let us use your career as an example. Assuming one of the big brands had invited photographers to work with them on their upcoming launch. Interested photographers were required to have a brief face-to-face meeting with the brand's marketing manager so that they could determine whether one was a good fit for the project or not. In this scenario, whether you get the project is beyond you. What is in your control or how you could make things better is by making sure that you are prepared by doing the due diligence investigations about the company, ensuring that you show up on time on the date, and ensuring that you are presentable, among other things. While this may not guarantee that you will get the project, it may slightly influence their decision. I say this because sometimes, people make decisions based on the small things we do. For example, if you were late for the meeting, they would interpret that the same may happen on the day of the launch." he had said.

Daniella had walked to the fireplace and had seemed to enjoy the smell of wood and the crackling sound it had made as it burned. She then turned her head to face Mr. Antonio's direction and said, "That seems to make a lot of sense. But, out of curiosity, how would you have used this method in the story you shared about your ex-girlfriend?"

Mr. Antonio had stood up and joined her at the fireplace. They had been standing close to each other, evidently enjoying the warmth from the dancing flames. "Going back to my story, most of the arguments had sprouted because of my negligence in listening to her and understanding that she was a perfectionist. Little things like not putting my socks in the right place irritated her. I should have paid more attention and become better at that, thus preventing arguments. On the other hand, the tone she used when correcting me had been beyond my control, and I should have acknowledged that that was her way of reacting to such things. It was my responsibility not to counter her reaction but to respond instead."

Daniella had then murmured, "Isn't reacting and responding the same thing?" as she rubbed her hands back and forth quickly.

"Not at all," Mr. Antonio had said, walking back to the couch. Daniella had followed him, and Mr. Antonio had continued, "when you react to something, you tend to act in the moment and match the energy in the room without considering the consequences.

A reaction is more of a defense mechanism. It gets characterized by biased judgments. On the other hand, a response allows one to consider the best way to deal with any given situation. I would recommend that the next time you feel stressed over something, to take a moment and flip the script and ask yourself those simple questions." he had said.

Daniella did not have any further questions, and they finished their session. Mr. Antonio had walked her to the door and had bid her goodbye.

Last Session with Mr. Antonio

Daniella booked another session with Mr. Antonio one month after the stress management session. She had walked into his office wearing a bright yellow sundress that matched her handbag and shoes. After the pleasantries, she reached into her bag, removed the book he had lent her, and thanked him for the gesture. Mr. Antonio smiled, pointed to the bookshelf using his right index finger, and told her that she was welcome to select another book of her choice. Again, Daniella smiled and thanked him. Next, Mr. Antonio asked her if she wanted to discuss any topic or issue. In response, she nodded sideways and said a simple "No." Mr. Antonio had then asked her if she was happy to use that session as a reflection session, and Daniella nodded in agreement. He then decided that they would start by taking a tour down memory lane and asked her to describe what had made her seek out his services.

"I was going through a mixed feeling phase in my life. I had lost meaning in the things that mattered most to me. Things like my work and spending time with family. I knew something amiss was going on within me, but I could not put my hands on it. Sometimes I felt like all was good, but other times I felt like the universe was conspiring against me. I came to you at the recommendation of my fiancée, a man I believe in and know has nothing but the best interests and intentions for me. He reminded me there was no shame in asking for help from an expert if I wanted to feel happy and content. I was unsure if I needed the help as I did not think anything was wrong with me. Besides, I had always managed to solve my past issues and did not see the need to waste my hard-earned money on someone. So, I held onto the mentality that everything was unfolding as expected despite the odd days. I came to you for two reasons, and now that I look back, they were stupid reasons." she laughed. "One, I was trying to prove a point to Jacob by showing him that I did not need help and I was perfectly okay, and two, I did not want him to think otherwise or less of me." she had said, and then leaned forward and picked her cup of cappuccino that Mr. Antonio's assistant had prepared for them.

"Daniella, I still remember our discovery session when you first came to me. I could see in your body language that you never wanted to be there. You checked your watch most of the time we were having that conversation. Yet, despite all that, I saw an ambitious woman lost in her world through our conversation. You held so much power at the time that it was slowly consuming you. You knew what you wanted but had no idea how to express yourself or manage it. Honestly, you were a puzzle that I was hoping to get to work with, and the day I received the appointment notice from my assistant, I knew great days were ahead. Today, I am happy to say I see a tremendous difference, and I am super proud of you." he had said in a lighthearted way. He had then asked her to summarize what progress she had witnessed since she had started working with him in a nutshell.

"Honestly, I feel like I have been born again, literally speaking. The Daniella of today is making decisions that are close to her heart. She speaks her mind out, is laughing more, and shock on me, I do own tears." she had laughed. "I have mended most relationships that I thought lost, and my business is in a much better place." she had said enthusiastically. "I am glad to hear of that progress, Daniella; I have also observed some changes in you. For instance, your word phrases have shifted from 'I can't, and It is not possible' to 'I will give it a try" and many other statements. I must say, Daniella, you are transforming into the butterfly in your story." he had said with a grin on his face. "All these thanks to you for your generosity with knowledge and your eagerness to deliver nothing but quality work." Daniella had said, matching the grin Mr. Antonio had.

"Ooh no, all these thanks to your efforts, motivation, consistency, and acceptance of the change. As I have always told you, change only occurs when we accept to shift our mindsets from fixed mindsets to growth or resilient mindsets. When we allow and embrace change, our lives tend to take a turn, and we start witnessing great things happening in our lives, no matter how small they are. I am just a vessel to guide and point you in the right direction." Mr. Antonio had said.

Next, they discussed what Daniella needed to do to avoid falling back into old habits. Mr. Antonio knew human beings would tend to fall back into old patterns as were familiar territories and almost one's default settings as there was always comfort in what one knew and worry in unfamiliar things. Mr. Antonio had been curious to hear what Daniella had planned for the days ahead. In response, she said, using hand gestures, "Well, I have a couple of things in mind. Firstly, I will continue journaling, as since I started, I have realized that I can identify self-triggers, my strengths, and areas that need improvement. I have also realized that I am working smart and not hard, saving extra time for friends and family. Secondly, I will maintain my committee members as they have been great assets. I am now past the awkward phase of conducting imaginary meetings with them. Thirdly, I plan to practice mindfulness, which will help me become aware of my thoughts, feelings, and actions. I will do this by paying attention to my five senses and making meditation a regular thing. Fourthly, I will replace the habits I want to stop with new habits. For instance, instead of ghosting people I thought had offended me, I will continue to be the bigger person and reach out to clear the air with them. And finally, I will continue reciting my morning affirmations and believe in them. My favorite affirmation is that I am worthy of love from others and have great support around me. I am calling this the new branding for Daniella, " she said with a big smile.

Mr. Antonio was impressed with Daniella's master plan and informed her that that had been just the foundation. As time passed by, she would find herself formulating more ideas. To conclude their session, Mr. Antonio gave her the story of the dragonfly insect. "I know at some point you have seen or heard about the dragonfly. In almost every part of the world, you will find the dragonfly near body waters, and I am sure you, as a child, did play around with them at some point. However, there are certain features I would like to highlight to you. One, a dragonfly's scurrying flight across water, reminds us to always go beyond what is visible to the naked eye and investigate the deeper aspects of life. Two, a dragonfly's body and wings reflect life as it moves across water depending on the angle of the sun's rays, and this reminds us that as the sun rises, each day will present different things that we should embrace and strive to discover our abilities. By doing so, we can discover our abilities through the inner soul search that unmasks our authentic selves, eliminating doubts that we self-cast on our identities over the years. Three, most people do not know that the dragonfly only flies for a fraction of its life during the nymph stage. While this may sound alarming, it does remind us to live in the moment and create more joy in our lives; thus, one is aware of who they are, what they are up to, the direction to follow, et cetera, and not live in the shadows as living in the shadows allow other people's achievements and greatness to cover our own. It also symbolizes living beyond the blocks that limit one's growth and capability to grow and blossom. Finally, their large compound eyes symbolize our ability to visualize and see beyond the blocks we have installed on ourselves. Too many communities globally, dragonflies are a symbol of hope and change." he had said.

Daniella had been fascinated with the story and had told Mr. Antonio, "It is amazing how much we can learn from insects and animals' lives."

Mr. Antonio smiled back and said, "You are right, Daniella, and I want you to remember the stories I have told you during our time together. They are stories with great lessons that we can apply in our lives. They will help sharpen your thoughts and enable you to look at things differently." Daniella thanked Mr. Antonio for the great insights and for allowing her to discover herself better. Mr. Antonio had also mentioned to Daniella that she had a free bonus session that she could redeem anytime. Daniella had smiled, thanked him for his generosity, and had then bid him goodbye.

The Party Planning

Towards the end of the year, around October, the town was beautifully decorated with flowers. Every person you met on the street had a smile on their face. The big day was finally here. Call the fashion police! Everyone was in their best outfit. Some had had their outfits purposely made for this event, though they would not admit it.

Firstly, before we dive into the details of the party, allow me to take you back on how events unfolded after the last session with Mr. Antonio. Daniella had felt empowered by Mr. Antonio's words and sessions. She understood that she was in control of her destiny. She understood that she was unique and did not need to be good at everything. Just like a fish cannot climb a tree and a lion cannot swim as well as a fish, she knew there was something special about her. Like an eagle that does not feed on dead things, she was determined to let the past be. She was focused on the present and hoping for a better future, leaving the past where it belonged. With the help of her newly formed committee, Daniella was feeling better. Whenever she met a stumbling block, she would schedule a meeting and listen to their insights; Rosa, who had appointed herself as the planner for the invite-only party, was growing restless as she wanted to have the guest list. Each time Daniella asked her to be patient, reassuring her that she was working on it. Rosa had wondered why Daniella was complicating things as she believed it would be easy for a celebrity to come up with a list.

During one of her imaginary meetings, she decided to cancel the rumor of an invite-only party and instead invite everyone to her wedding party. Before coming to that decision, Daniella was confused and unsure if she was making the right decision by inviting only a select few people. Being a flourishing businessman, Jacob had made it clear that the budget was not a problem. She could go all in if she wanted to, as he wanted to give her the best wedding. Whatever she decided to do, he was in support of it. Daniella called for an imaginary meeting, and then her imaginary committee members gave her insights that convinced her it was a good idea to invite everyone if that was what her heart desired. The imaginary meeting went as follows:

The first committee member had been confidence, "Daniella, I know you are afraid of what some people will say when they see your guests from the unique 100 lists. I want to remind you that this is your day, and if anybody has a problem with anyone, they should leave. That should not bother you as you cannot make everyone happy. I know deep down you feel that this is the right thing to do, and I want you to follow your gut feeling. Besides Daniella, with me by your side, what could go wrong? I know it is cliché me to repeat the story of the bird on the branch, but there are great lessons to be learned from there on my capabilities.

As you remember, in the story, a bird landed on a tree branch and enjoyed the view and the protection from other dangerous animals on the ground. However, a strong wind swayed so hard that it seemed like the branch where the bird had landed would break from the tree's trunk and fall. Despite all these odds, the bird did not move or panic; instead, the bird continued sitting on the tree branch as it knew if it came to worse, it could fly away and save itself from the fall or move to other branches and continue watching the beautiful view. Just like the bird Daniella, when it comes down to making the tough decision, while the idea of drama and ridicule may be strong, look deeply from within and believe that whatever choice you make is what you desire and do that with your head high."

Next was forgiveness: "Well, it depends if her heart is pure and she has genuinely forgiven those who wronged her. You are not doing them a favor when you forgive someone and mean it. Instead, you are setting yourself free by releasing that burden, which brings you peace of mind. Forgiving someone is not easy, but it is the key to happiness. I am sure you remember the story of the angry bee that is told to children to remind them of the importance of forgiveness. As you can remember, a colony of bees lived together in a tall tree. They always did things together, from playing to working. Often when they were moving, they would accidentally bump into each other. Still, they would always apologize to one another and continue with their activities happily. One day two bees bumped into each other, one bee apologized, but the other bee got angry and went and sat alone on a branch waiting for the other bee to feel guilty. The day went by, and the other bees continued their activities. In fact, at one point, some other bees came and invited the angry bee to join them, but he refused. As the day progressed, the angry bee started to feel sad and missed flying with the other bees. Then he thought he could be happy again and do his favorite stuff; all he had to do was forgive and let it go. He thought about it, and off he went and was happy again.

You see, Daniella; forgiveness helps ease the burden we hold in our hearts. So, deciding whom to invite should not be that hard, considering you do not have any grudges. Besides, sometimes we lose time worrying about things that are just in our minds instead of doing things that matter to us. Sometimes when you put yourself in the shoes of another, you get to see things from a different perspective. Like in this story, the other bee did not feel any guilt as it was an accident, and he had done his part by apologizing."

The next committee member, honesty, had said, "Time to speak the truth, Daniella. Have you forgiven and let by-gone be by-gone?" and in response, Daniella had said, "Yes, I have forgiven and forgotten. But…and it was then happiness had said, "Ooh no Daniella, there is no room for but. It is either a yes or no question. I want you to glow on your big day, and if there is anyone you feel will stop you from that, then do not invite them. It is your day, girl. Like forgiveness said in the beautiful story, I glow better when you refuse to let things hold you down. My competitor's sadness is a block away, and always ready to step in. I have seen sadness manipulate others, and I do not want that to be the case for you. Worry is the middle name for sadness, and I promise you, you might end up not enjoying the day when it manages to sneak inside you."

Ambition had then asked Daniella, "Let me try and phrase it differently; what do you desire to achieve by inviting everyone?" At this point, Daniella recalled one session with Mr. Antonio where he had introduced to her the concept of outcome frame that focused on establishing her end goal and another concept that he had called ecology check. With ecology check, he had explained to her that it involved checking the consequences of any plans or goals.

The next committee member had been self-awareness, "O-oh! O-oh! Ambition is doing it again, but there are great points, Daniella; what standards do you want to convey on the day? In fact, let me add something else here; I want you, before you answer us, to visualize these two scenarios. Scenario one, let us assume that you invited everyone to the wedding; What is the worst that would happen? And scenario two, let us assume that you had a private wedding with a guest list; what is the worst that would happen?" Daniella said, "Those are tough questions but great insights too.

As you know, I have reached out to nearly everyone I had listed, and we are on good terms with the majority. I have let go of the grudges I held against them, and yes, you are right; with forgiveness, I feel lighter and happier. Thinking about the last two questions, in both scenarios, my goal is to have a memorable day with no worry. Inviting everyone might worry me during the wedding as I am not sure of my guests' rapport with each other. On the other hand, inviting a select few will still cause me to worry as I know I will start feeling bad and guilty about those I did not invite. I honestly want the day to mark a fresh start in my life, and with that, I mean to avoid worrying about things beyond me.

The subsequent committee member self-control had said, as the chairman of this committee, I see that you are at a crossroads. Both outcomes have a worst scenario that you have tagged on them. One thing that I picked out from those statements is that you are worried about other people's feelings, and to me, that is a distraction. As you make your decision, I want you to focus on your goals for the day. Forget the distractions and become in control of yourself. Your feelings should be the priority. Let us hear what honor and coordination have to say; despite coming in late for the meeting, I am sure they have good insights.

Next, honor added, "In one of our meetings Daniella, you asked me what it meant to be an honorable person. So today, I will give you two words: be genuine. If making this decision has no malicious intentions, you are on the right path. Be the person you say you are to the world. I will also emphasize concentrating on your goals for the day. Once those are clear, the rest should be as easy as ABC. Besides, what has convinced you that those two outcomes will be the reality? Do you have any evidence?" after which coordination added, " As always, they save the best for last. Daniella, when you wrote to me inviting me to join your committee, you wanted me to assist you with having a balance between your three brains, the head, gut, and heart. I have empowered you over time, and now I want you to focus and listen to what all three have to say. I want you to stop concentrating on the big things and listen to the small details they tell you; you will find better clarity in the minor information and facts. As I always say, there is power in paying attention to the small details."

Finally, self-control ended the meeting and said, " Well, Daniella, you have heard our thoughts and insights, and it is time for you to reflect and make your decision. Make us proud. And with that, I call the meeting to an end."

The morning following the meeting, Daniella called Rosa and asked her to invite everyone to her wedding. She was okay with who would attend, nor what may or may not happen. Instead, she decided to focus on her main goal, which was to have an elegant wedding. While reflecting on the wisdom from her committee, she remembered another piece of knowledge from Mr. Antonio, where he had explained a formula for managing to overthink. In this formula, he had asked her to be a passive observant rather than an active observer when having thoughts that were troubling her. In this method, she could picture the anxious thoughts written on a banner pulled by an airplane and watch them fly around her mind without reacting to them. Alternatively, she could imagine the worries that were troubling her as bubbles that burst as they rose into her consciousness.

Further, she paid vital attention to what she considered a stressful situation and followed the method Mr. Antonio had taught her. With all this knowledge, Daniella resorted to doing what was best for her. Rosa was surprised as she was expecting a list for an invite-only party but happy that there was progress in the wedding planning, so she got to work.

The Wedding

It was an exciting month as it had also been Daniella's birthday month, and the wedding date had finally reached. The guests were settling in and ready to witness the union of the famous photographer and her flourishing businessman. The first stage of the wedding was the church ceremony. At precisely 10 am, the guests had settled down, the groom and the bridal line had made their entrance, and it was time for Daniella to join everyone. The big church doors opened, and it was evident that everyone was stunned by how stunning Daniella looked by their facial expressions and reactions. Her pearl wedding gown fitted her perfectly. Jacob flashed his biggest smile as he watched his bride walk towards him. The church ceremony had been kept short, and they moved to the reception soon after. They decorated Tora's club backyard to fit the occasion with bright cantaloupe color with a touch of light blue. As one walked into the reception area, photographers encouraged them to leave a short message for the newlyweds on camera. The entrance got tagged the red-carpet corner as the guests received the red-carpet treatment, and boy, oh boy! How people love to be on camera. The photographers had a hard job maintaining order.

On the other side, the chefs had set up the meals, and there was more than enough to feed all the guests and more. The decorators dressed the reception tables in cool white linen and neatly placed the cutlery on them. They also customized the napkins with the newlyweds' pictures showing the places they had visited globally. The wedding committee had gone above and beyond. Since they knew the confirmed guests in attendance, they had set up the venue to accommodate that number and ensure the place looked manageable.

Lots of dancing and speech-making continued through to the evening reception. The expressions on Daniella's parents clearly stated that they were proud of their daughter and the woman she had become. Daniella's heart warmed as she watched their guests having a great time. The newlyweds were excused later in the night to go and rest as they prepared to leave for their honeymoon. Rosa did a beautiful job in the planning and got tagged as the modern wedding planner. Being Daniella's best friend, it was easy for her to make decisions, as she knew her friends' tastes and preferences.

Further, with her wedding approaching soon, she was preparing herself, and helping Daniella's big day had given her much insight. After driving their parents' home, Jack and Rosa joined the rest of his siblings at Zee's condo. They spent the night celebrating that their baby sister was finally married to a man she loved. They spent the night reminiscing about Daniella's past. Then, Yeli landed in the spotlight with questions about her dating life out loud, bluntly, and outrightly. Yeli being a private person, dodged the bullet by pretending to be drunk, and they called it a night.

After her honeymoon, Daniella managed to go through the gifts from her friends, colleagues, fans, and loved ones. It was then that Daniella had come across Mr. Antonio's gift, and the card had read:

Dear Daniella,

First, congratulations on your big day. I am sure you made a beautiful bride, and Jacob is lucky to have you as a wife. I am grateful that we got to work together, and I hope all our sessions have significantly impacted your life. Daniella, I want you to remember that you are a butterfly who has broken out of the cocoon and is ready to explore what the world has to offer. There will be stormy days, and there will be days when the sun will shine bright. Whatever the season, I want you to keep going and never stop. Each season has its purpose, and you either win or learn from each one. But remember, if you look closely, no matter the circumstances, there is always an opportunity of learning a lesson in disguise.

Distance yourself from feelings of failure, rejection, hatred, and other negative thoughts that might be creeping into your mind. Pass down these values to your children so they may pass them on to future generations. Remember our sessions, and don't stop with the morning affirmations or the late-night meetings with your committee. Whenever you feel a non-desired trait is coming in, please write a letter addressing it, and after enjoy watching it burn to ashes. You are in control, Daniella.

I present to you this painting; on the edges, you will notice the life cycle of a butterfly, and in the middle, it is blank. I specifically asked for this design as I want you to remember that each day represents a blank space in your book, and only you have the power to write your story. Furthermore, the butterfly's life cycle is a reminder of the seasons. Whenever you face darker days, that should give you hope that brighter days are coming.

My door is always open if you need any of my insights and guidance. I have also sent you five books that will impact your journey. I wish you the very best, Daniella.

Also, please accept my apology for not making it to the wedding and informing you at the last minute. As you may have heard, I got nominated for best coach of the year. As a finalist, my presence in the United Kingdom surfaced, and the date of the awards was the same as your wedding ceremony. Wish me luck!

That's it for now,

Antonio

The Bonus Session with Mr. Antonio

One year after her wedding, Daniella thought it was time to cash in the bonus session. They had exchanged pleasantries, after which Daniella had said, "Mr. Antonio, I have so much to share with you, and yet we have a limited time slot. So, I will keep it brief and to the point. First, congratulations on winning the best coaches award last year. You deserved it; I am a living testimony of your wondrous works. Please continue impacting our lives through your wisdom, as clarity on our path is necessary for us to thrive and live our authentic lives. I know you hear this a lot Mr. Antonio, but I cannot stop emphasizing your remarkable work.

After our last session, there was a lot of pressure left and right regarding the invite-only party and my wedding ceremony. It was through committee meetings with my imaginary members and reference to some of our sessions that I got the brilliant idea to invite everyone to my wedding ceremony and cancel the rumors of the invite-only party. After all, they were rumors seeing as I had not made any public announcement. Days towards the wedding ceremony, I received some apology gifts and emails from a select group that I hoped would make it, as I had considered them part of my close-knit family professionally. At first, I was annoyed as it was clear they had sat down and discussed and made a consistent decision not to attend the ceremony. But again, I remembered that you once told me never to make assumptions as everyone makes the best choices available to them at the time. With that mentality, I convinced myself that it was for the best, as there is an unconscious positive intention behind every behavior.

The wedding ceremony was beautiful. Initially, I was worried there would be drama; however, Jacob reminded me to carry a positive attitude as we tend to attract what our unconscious mind has in store. Further, in one of my committee meetings, we devised a solution. We decided that I would create a specific morning affirmation that would get recited each day until the wedding date. Each morning for a month before the wedding, I recited the words; there would be no drama on my wedding day. I would take a few minutes to visualize the day and how our guests will fill it with laughter and love. Finally, the wedding date came, and it was as beautiful as I had imagined. There was no sign of drama, and the paparazzi were kind enough to feature all the best moments.

After our honeymoon, it took some time to catch up with what I had missed out on during the last couple of months leading to the wedding. Being a business owner, one must pay attention to all the details as that may cost them a fortune. After catching up with work-related stuff, I decided to send a thank-you gift to all those who made it to the wedding and those who sent in their apologies. Mr. Antonio, I am glad I did not hold any grudges against the select group who sent in their apologies. As it turned out, they were protecting me. One group member had fallen ill, and they were taking shifts looking after her. As a group of ten people, they had agreed that seven would attend the ceremony, and the remainder would take shifts looking after her. On the weekend of my wedding ceremony, she was to be in India for a procedure. Since she had no family around, they volunteered to go with her. Gratefully she is well now and back on her feet. After learning all this, I was proud of myself for not ruining my big day with negative thoughts that were not justifiable. This experience taught me to only judge one's actions after understanding their reason.

My relationship has also improved with ninety percent of the people from the 100 list. Some of us are in business together, while others have become cocktail buddies. We have made a point of meeting at least once a month to catch up, which has impacted my life, as all the negative emotions I once held are gone. A space has been created inside me, filling me with positive things. It feels good when you are not constantly worried about something; instead, when faced with challenging situations, you decide to think beyond them.

For instance, my latest gallery exhibition, in my employees' eyes, was a disaster. We planned to do a freebie competition which went out with the advertisement posters, which were supposed to be announced by a famous pop star. We got fully booked, and we had to turn away some people. On the date of the event, our guest, the pop star, was a no-show; according to his agent, he was double booked. I almost hit the panic button as I could see the negative tweets going up with the guests expressing their disappointments. The pop star was the real deal, and so, due to disappointments, the incredible artwork exhibited went almost unnoticed. I then remembered that there was no bad publicity, and they had every right to express their frustrations. I quickly cashed in a favor from a friend who is an artist, and he was more than happy to step in at the last minute and save the day. Two days after the exhibition, the pop star's agency tweeted and apologized to everyone who was at the exhibition. They promised to make it up to them. We are organizing another exhibition where the pop star will perform for free. Those who attended the last exhibition will get a free pass. And this turned out to be a win-win situation for everyone. I also gained new prospects from the negative tweets that went viral. I guess hitting the panic button is never the answer.

Jacob and I are planning to start our family next year. I am excited to be a mother. I cannot wait to teach my children the virtue of positivity, embracing a mindset shift, and looking at stressful situations as opportunities. I want my children to embrace their uniqueness and accept themselves as they are. I hope they do not get to the nightmare of the monster as I did but instead dream of themselves soaring high each day. I promise to bring them around for you to say hello to them.

Mr. Antonio, I am grateful for your insights. I usually did the talking during our sessions, but you held my hands through your insightful questions. Today, I am a better version of myself, and I pray that God grants you a long life to continue impacting the lives of others as you did with mine.

Ooh! Before I forget, I loved your wedding gift, it is hanging in my study room, and each time I look at it, all the wisdom from our sessions comes flowing down. A bright future awaits me, and I cannot wait to fill in the blank pages.

The End

Words from the Author

Dear Reader,

Congratulations on taking the time to enrich your mindset growth. I am confident that this book has helped you revisit some areas, if not all, in your life and that you have, hopefully, started on the journey of self-healing and growth by re-authoring the limiting stories that you hold dear. I have poured my heart out to you through the characters in this book. I have also applied my knowledge from life experience and my coaching expertise.

When I wrote this book, I had you who were not pursuing their full potential because of the mental blocks you have created in your mind. I know they exist because I have been there and lived that life. While it has been a journey to get to where I am today, it is possible, and all you have to do is accept that you are unique and in charge. Further, you do not need to run a company to become a CEO; you are a company already. So, the next time someone asks what you do, make sure to quote confidently that you are the CEO of your life. By implanting this statement in your life, you find yourself striving and working hard to make better versions of yourself a reality each day.

Finally, be aware of your habits because sometimes we are so used to doing things in a particular way that we do not realize how that pattern affects our outcomes. For example, make it a habit to question your moves by assessing whether you are using the best resources available. Remember, there is no shame in asking for help. I overcame my limiting beliefs because I accepted vulnerability and dropped my fences.

Hey, you are the CEO and director of your life, take charge and make the best decisions for yourself today.

With so much love, Jane

Printed in Great Britain
by Amazon

30106643R00079